A Guide to the

National Curriculum

Fourth Edition

Bob Moon

OXF[ORD]
UNIVERSI[TY]

OXFORD
UNIVERSITY PRESS

Great Clarendon Street, Oxford OX2 6DP

Oxford University Press is a department of the University of Oxford.
It furthers the University's objective of excellence in research, scholarship,
and education by publishing worldwide in

Oxford New York
Auckland Bangkok Bogotá Buenos Aires Cape Town
Chennai Dar es Salaam Delhi Florence Hong Kong Istanbul Karachi
Kolkata Kuala Lumpur Madrid Melbourne Mexico City Mumbai Nairobi
Paris São Paulo Shanghai Taipei Tokyo Toronto Warsaw

Oxford is a registered trade mark of Oxford University Press
in the UK and in certain other countries

First published 1991
Second edition 1994
Third edition 1996
Fourth edition 2001

3 5 7 9 10 8 6 4 2

British Library Cataloguing in Publication Data

Data available

ISBN 0 19 838290 1

Printed in Great Britain by
Cox & Wyman Ltd, Reading, Berkshire

Contents

4

Acknowledgements

A wide range of people has contributed to the information contained in this guide. These include officers from the councils and agencies that have overseen the National Curriculum since 1988 and officials of the Department for Education and Employment (DfEE).

Many colleagues from the Open University have also contributed to the various editions. This edition has benefitted from specialist subject contributors who provided full drafts of various chapters. These include:

Sandra Amos and Richard Boohan (science)
Hilary Bourdillon (history)
Ian Eyres (literacy and numeracy)
Linda Haggarty (mathematics)
Steve Hutchinson and Ann Shelton Mayes (testing and assessment)
Jenny Leach and Anne Storey (English)
Gwyneth Owen-Jackson (design and technology)
Maggie Smith (geography)
Gary Spruce (music)
Martin Workman (modern foreign languages)

These contributions were invaluable in providing up-to-date information and interpretation in specialist areas. Sharron Jenkinson of Oxfordshire LEA drafted the chapter on Inclusion. Julie Herbert, as ever, provided the necessary administrative and secretarial support. Finally, I would like to thank Barbara Vander, who first suggested that a guide such as this would be of interest and value, particularly to those coming new to the National Curriculum.

Bob Moon

Oxford, January 2001

Introduction

The National Curriculum was first introduced in 1988. It is the public and legal statement about the curriculum that every child should study between the ages of five and sixteen. It is important for teachers and parents to understand the structure and terminology of the National Curriculum as a whole and the individual subjects within it. This is particularly so for teachers in training and for the thousands of parents playing an active role on governing bodies and parent–teacher associations.

This guide:

■ provides an introduction to the way the National Curriculum is organized in primary, middle, and secondary schools;

■ explains the meanings of the terms used on a daily basis now by teachers and by pupils;

■ outlines the content of the different subjects;

■ gives guidance on the systems of assessment and testing used;

■ sets out the entitlement parents have in relation to information about their child's progress.

In using this guide, three important points need to be borne in mind. First, it does not attempt to serve as a substitute for the official regulations, and formal documentation associated with the National Curriculum. Some of the documentation is daunting, even for the interested reader, but it does set out the statutory basis to which teachers and schools must work. This new edition covers the National Curriculum for the period 2000–2005. The Government's aim is to keep the requirements unaltered over that period. Earlier versions went through almost annual changes, a process confusing to teachers, pupils, and parents. But there may be minor alterations, and it is important to stress the importance of referring to official publications for the precise legal situation at any one time or in respect of a particular age group. These publications are quite expensive, but all schools keep copies and can make them available to parents.

The official web sites are a further source of reference, and a number of useful web-site addresses are included in the further information section at the end of this guide. A National Curriculum now exists in England, Northern Ireland and Wales. Scotland has different arrangements. This guide focusses primarily on the requirements in England, although examples of the Northern Irish and Welsh requirements are given in the description of subjects such as design and technology and history. A lot of the curriculum structure and terminology is common across the three countries, but reference should be made to the specific orders for each country, which can be found on the official web sites listed at the end of this guide.

A second point is that the Labour government elected in 1997, whilst retaining the National Curriculum, has introduced in England and Wales a series of advisory strategies for schools, which, whilst technically outside the formal National Curriculum, have almost equal significance. This is most significant for primary and secondary schools in the areas of literacy and numeracy. This guide now has a chapter on the primary National Literacy and Numeracy Strategies and discussion of the secondary equivalent can be found at the end of the sections on English and mathematics. These strategies do undergo change, and reference to up-to-date information is important. The Department for Education and Employment web site (see the further information section for the address) should be referred to in the first instance. There is also a national specification for a pre-school foundation stage of curriculum or equivalent. This is not part of the statutory National Curriculum. Information, however, is included in Chapter Four to provide an indication of the experience children are expected to have prior to entering the formal period of schooling.

This leads to a third point. The information and guidance set out in this guide should be supplemented by contact and involvement with schools. Early experience with the National Curriculum showed that schools require greater flexibility to interpret the requirements than was envisaged in 1988. Changes have been introduced to permit this. Despite the political and educational difficulties in introducing the National Curriculum, a central core of curriculum opportunities and entitlement for all children is now enshrined in law. There is political support for this across all major political parties.

What is the National Curriculum?

Values, aims, and purposes

The Education Act of 1996, section 351, requires that all maintained schools (that is schools funded by the Government) are required to provide a balanced and broad-based curriculum that:

- promotes the spiritual, moral, cultural, mental and physical development of pupils at the school and in society;

- prepares pupils at the school for the opportunities, responsibilities and experiences of adult life.

Everyone in the education system, particularly the Secretary of State for Education and Employment, local authorities, governing bodies and head teachers, are required to take steps to achieve these requirements. A key task for the Secretary of State is to provide a national framework for the curriculum in which the prescribed, statutory, National Curriculum is of central importance.

The National Curriculum from 2000 fulfils this requirement first by suggesting the values and purposes underpinning the school curriculum. Education is seen as influencing and reflecting the values of society and the kind of society that it is hoped will develop in the future. Examples of such values are given under the headings:

- *the self* (for example, develop self-respect and self-discipline)
- *relationships* (for example, care for others and exercise goodwill in our dealings with them)
- *society* (for example, recognise that the love and commitment required for a secure and happy childhood can also be found in families of different kinds)

■   *the environment* (for example, accept our responsibility to maintain a sustainable environment for future generations).

For schools to respond successfully to such values, the National Curriculum documentation sets out two aims that are derived from the Education Act of 1996.

Aim 1:   The school curriculum should aim to provide opportunities for all pupils to learn and achieve.

Aim 2:   The school curriculum should aim to promote pupils' spiritual, moral, social and cultural development and prepare all pupils for the opportunities, responsibilities and experience of life.

Each of these aims is elaborated upon. Aim 1, for example, includes the need for pupils to appreciate human aspirations and achievements in aesthetics, scientific, technological and social fields. Aim 2 includes the importance of equipping pupils as consumers to make informed judgements and independent decisions and to understand their responsibilities and rights.

Officially, the National Curriculum is seen as having four main purposes:

■   *to establish an entitlement*
     all pupils are entitled, whatever their background, to be taught the National Curriculum

■   *to establish standards*
     explicit statements about the standards that can be achieved allow for ambitious target setting: for pupils and for schools

■   *to promote continuity and coherence*
     allowing progression for the pupils within and between the schools they attend

■   to promote public understanding
     creating the basis for public confidence in schools.

The structure of the National Curriculum

In order to understand the National Curriculum you will first need to become familiar with a small number of terms and phrases. These are fairly straightforward and are used on a daily basis in schools.

Key stages

The National Curriculum is required by law to be taught to pupils in all maintained or local authority schools. It is organised on the basis of four key stages:

	Pupils' age range	School year groups
Key stage 1	5–7	1–2
Key stage 2	7–11	3–6
Key stage 3	11–14	7–9
Key stage 4	14–16	10–11

The phrase 'key stage' is now used frequently by teachers, for example when explaining to parents how the curriculum is organised and, at the end of a key stage, when reporting on the progress a pupil has made.

Core subjects and non-core foundation subjects

The National Curriculum is described in terms of twelve subjects. Most of the subjects, such as English, mathematics and science, the three *core subjects*, are well known and have featured in the school curriculum for many years. A few in the list of *non-core foundation subjects* are less familiar, such as 'citizenship' which was introduced in 2000. Over the past few decades, some subjects have been brought together under new titles. Anyone, for example, who studied home economics, metalwork or woodwork at school will find elements of each of these under design and technology. The National Curriculum subjects are listed on the next page.

Core subjects	Non-core foundation subjects
English	Design and Technology
Mathematics	Information and communication technology
Science	History
(Note: in Wales Welsh is taught as a core subject where the medium of instruction in a school is Welsh. In all other Welsh schools it is one of the non-core foundation subjects.)	Geography
	Modern foreign languages
	Art and design
	Music
	Physical education
	Citizenship

Schools do not have to teach every subject in each of the key stages. In key stages 1 and 2, the primary years, citizenship and modern foreign languages are not required to be taught. At key stage 3 all twelve are required, whereas in key stage 4 (the GCSE years), schools and pupils have a smaller number of subjects that are legally required to be taught, to allow the inclusion of other options. Examples of such options can range from the traditional classics Latin or Greek to (more commonly) vocational or vocationally related subjects.

National Curriculum subjects required to be taught at key stage four:

English	Information and communication
Mathematics	technology
Science	Modern foreign languages
Design and technology	Physical education
	Citizenship

Key stage 4 is rather more complex than the other key stages, particularly as the National Curriculum links directly to the GCSE and other qualifications. The impact of this will be considered in Chapters 3 and 4, where we look at each of the subjects in turn.

Programmes of study

The *programmes of study* are legally binding statements that set out first the *knowledge, skills and pupil understanding* that must be taught during each key stage where each subject is taught; and second the *breadth of study*, that is the contexts, activities, areas of study and range of experiences through which knowledge, skills and understanding are taught. This may sound a rather complex formulation but the distinction becomes apparent when the programmes of study are examined. For example, at key stage 3, in English, under knowledge, skills and understanding pupils must be taught to:

> *speak fluently and appropriately in different contexts, adapting their talk for a range of purposes and audiences.*

The programme of study goes on to indicate how this should be done. Pupils should be taught to:

> *structure their talk clearly, using markers so that their listeners can follow the line of thought.*

Under breadth of study it indicates that the purposes of developing effective speaking should include:

> *describing, narrating, explaining, arguing, persuading, entertaining.*

In planning their teaching, teachers have to ensure that both the knowledge, skills and understanding, and the breadth of study requirements are covered.

Attainment targets and level descriptions

Here the terminology becomes rather more technical. Each subject of the National Curriculum has one or more *attainment targets* which set out the knowledge, skills and understanding which pupils of different abilities and maturities are expected to have by the end of each key stage. In English, for example, there are three attainment targets for: speaking and listening, reading, and writing.

Each of these attainment targets is divided up into eight *levels* (except citizenship – see Chapter 4). Most pupils would be expected to achieve level 2 by the age of 7. Below is the level 2 *level description* for the speaking and listening attainment target.

> *Pupils begin to show confidence in talking and listening, particularly where the topics interest them. On occasions, they show awareness of the needs of the listener by including relevant detail. In developing and explaining their ideas they speak clearly and use a growing vocabulary. They usually listen carefully and respond with increasing appropriateness to what others say. They are beginning to be aware that in some situations a more formal vocabulary and tone of voice are used.*

By the age of eleven most pupils will, for the same attainment target, be expected to reach level 4, as detailed below.

> *Pupils talk and listen with confidence in an increasing range of contexts. Their talk is adapted to the purpose: developing ideas thoughtfully, describing events and conveying their opinions clearly. In discussion, they listen carefully, making contributions and asking questions that are responsive to others' ideas and views. They use appropriately some of the features of standard English vocabulary and grammar.*

In all the subjects studied, most pupils will be expected to achieve level 2 at age 7, level 4 at age 11 and level 5 or 6 at age 14. What level they achieve is determined by national tests and teacher assessment. How this is done will be looked at in detail in Chapter 5. The top levels 7 and 8 are assessed through GCSE examinations. For each of the attainment targets there is also a further ninth description of *exceptional performance* beyond level 8. This is to motivate and reward the highest-attaining pupils.

The official formulation about what level pupils should have achieved at the end of each key stage refers always to 'the expected attainment for the majority of pupils'. There will be some pupils with particular aptitudes who can move more quickly through the different levels of the attainment targets. Others, including some with certain special educational needs, who experience difficulties in learning may move more slowly. The National Curriculum is a key part of Government policies to increase standards continuously, and all schools and teachers will be striving to achieve this. However, the performance of individual pupils cannot be interpreted by reference to the levels achieved above. They must be interpreted in terms of their previous achievements and the overall context in which they are learning. Teachers have the expertise to explain and interpret achievement in the National Curriculum, and parents and others should always make contact with them, at formal parents' meetings or at other times when they want to review any individual's achievements in the National Curriculum subjects.

The *programmes of study, the attainment targets* and the divisions of each attainment target into eight *levels* are the framework around which teachers and schools must organise their curriculum in order to meet the requirements of the National Curriculum. For most parents and pupils it is the translation of this framework into the curriculum as taught which is the most visible sign of the National Curriculum in action. It is important to remember that the National Curriculum wording does have the force of law. The examples for speaking above are easily understood. In other areas, the way it is set out is more difficult for anyone other than those with specialist knowledge. Teachers have now had considerable experience of ensuring that they cover the requirements of the National Curriculum. National tests are set on the basis that such coverage has been achieved. Parents and others, therefore, can have confidence that the way each school's curriculum is organised, does meet the legal requirements.

Schemes of work

If you read the official documentation on the National Curriculum, you will see only indirect reference to *schemes of work*. These, however, are the documents that describe how a school is organising its curriculum to meet all the requirements of the National Curriculum. Schemes of work are not set out in a formal legally binding way. School contexts vary and teachers are given discretion to exercise their judgement about the way in which the different subjects are taught. Schools are required to have schemes of work and anyone interested in how the National Curriculum is being taught in a particular school should ask to see these. They are of more practical relevance, for example, in looking at how the teaching and learning of an individual child might develop, than the legal documentation. To assist teachers in planning, there are now national examples of such schemes of work in most subjects (see Chapter 8).

The school curriculum and the National Curriculum

In this first chapter the structure and framework of the National Curriculum has been described. In the remainder of the book we look at why a National Curriculum exists and we look in more detail at the way it is implemented. It is important to remember, however, that any school curriculum is more than the National Curriculum. Some subjects are not covered by the legal National Curriculum regulations. Religious education, for example, must be taught in all schools but the syllabus for this is agreed locally in consultation with representatives of all the major religious traditions. Parents can choose to withdraw their children from religious education lessons. All schools are expected to provide sex education appropriate to the age of the child, but the detailed content and nature of sex education is for schools to decide. In this area, also, parents can choose to withdraw their children from all or part of the teaching.

Schools are being encouraged to ensure that certain types of learning opportunities exist across the whole curriculum, not just in one subject area. The development of pupils' spiritual, moral, social and cultural development is stressed. For example, pupils should, through their study in school, acquire a respect for their own culture and that of others, an interest in other people's ways of doing things and a healthy curiosity about differences between cultures. How this is done is for schools and teachers to decide, but there are plentiful opportunities to do this within the National Curriculum (through history, for example) and outside (through religious education).

Careers education must be provided in all secondary schools and all schools should be promoting personal, social and health education. Official guidelines exist in these areas. They do not have the detailed legal basis of the National Curriculum, but schools have an obligation to cover these areas and the way they are provided is looked at and reported on when schools are inspected.

One of the developments that is encouraged in the teaching of the National Curriculum 2000–2005 is the promotion of *key skills* that appear across a range of subjects and the curriculum as a whole. The evidence suggests that personal effectiveness in home life depends on acquiring these skills. Schools are encouraged, therefore, to develop six key skills:

> *communication*
> *application of numbers*
> *information technology*
> *working with others*
> *improving personal/own learning and performance*
> *problem solving*

and five areas of thinking skills:

> *information processing skills*
> *reasoning skills*
> *enquiry skills*
> *creative thinking skills*
> *evaluation skills.*

These lists appear quite daunting and they do require considerable skills by teachers to plan the curriculum as a whole, as well as individual class teaching and learning. The Government also has other ambitions for developing work across the curriculum that reflects contemporary social and economic concerns (financial capability, enterprise and entrepreneurial skills with related learning and education for sustainable development are the four examples listed in the National Curriculum Handbook for Teachers). It is important to stress again that individual schools are given the responsibility to develop a curriculum which reflects these concerns and ensures that the requirements of the National Curriculum are met. To understand any specific school curriculum, or assess any pupil's progress through that curriculum, it is necessary to look at the school's curriculum documentation and, most importantly, to talk to the head teacher and teachers.

Why a National Curriculum?

Advocates of a National Curriculum can be found right across the political spectrum, and it is now clear that a National Curriculum will be part of the educational scene for the foreseeable future.

Differences between schools

For many educationists the logic that underpins the provision of free and compulsory schooling also extends to what is taught. In arguing for a National Curriculum, they point to glaring inconsistencies that used to exist between schools. In the same locality, one primary school might have had a fully worked-out science scheme, and another school no science scheme at all. Even if both schools did have plans for teaching science, there would be no guarantee that they would approach the subject in similar ways. One school might have attempted to achieve a balance between the different scientific disciplines (physics, chemistry, and biology). The other, however, could have leaned heavily on the tradition of nature study – the sort of primary science that most parents remember from their own schooldays. In other subjects similar differences existed. A survey by Her Majesty's Inspectorate just before the National Curriculum was introduced, showed how haphazard the teaching of history and geography could be. It pointed to the lack of any attempt in many schools to ensure that children came into contact with progressively more demanding ideas, skills, and concepts.

Inequality of provision

In secondary schools, the existence of different curriculum opportunities could be seen clearly before the introduction of the National Curriculum. Girls, for example, often chose to drop the physical sciences in favour of biology. Boys significantly outnumbered girls in the technology classes that became increasingly available in the decade prior to the introduction of the National Curriculum. In a similar way, boys had very little contact with home economics. The number of students opting to study modern languages through to the end of year 11 or 13 was considerably less than in other subjects, and overall standards naturally appeared lower than in many other European countries. A National Curriculum provides a framework that can rule out such inconsistencies and inequalities.

Raising standards

Many supporters of the National Curriculum were also motivated by the desire to improve the quality of schooling and raise standards. The debate over standards has attracted media interest and controversy for many years. Some people have perceived a fall in standards of attainment in subjects such as English and mathematics. This is vigorously refuted by others, who point to the regular improvements in examination performance of both 16- and 18-year-olds. Each year, the publication of GCSE and A level results receives national attention and, overall, in each year there has been a gradual improvement in standards. About half of all the GCSE subjects taken are now graded at the higher level A–C. At A level, over a third of school-leavers are now obtaining the grades to go on to university; thirty years ago it was less than 10 per cent.

Judging standards over time is a complex task. Knowledge is always evolving and the sorts of tasks and questions that are appropriate in one decade may be redundant in the next. Extending the comparisons over more than a decade gives even greater difficulties. Changes in language usage make comparisons in English difficult. In mathematics the pound, shillings, and pence sums familiar to some parents and grandparents could hardly be set today.

Despite the complexity and inconclusiveness of the debate, a political and media message about declining standards achieved widespread public acceptance. More than one Prime Minister has chosen to exploit the issue for political advantage. James Callaghan, in a famous speech, as far back as 1976, talked of his concern at finding 'complaints from industry that new recruits from the schools sometimes do not have the basic tools to do the job that is required'. Margaret Thatcher in her 1987 speech to the Conservative Party Conference made a direct link between schooling and economic success: 'To compete successfully in tomorrow's world – against Japan, Germany and the United States – we need well-educated, well-trained, creative young people. If education is backward today, the national performance will be backward tomorrow'. Tony Blair has made 'Education, Education, Education' his major manifesto commitment and has launched a crusade to raise standards.

International comparisons represent a further dimension of the standards debate. Yet again, there are difficulties in coming to conclusive judgements. Setting tests that are comparable across a range of different countries and cultures has proved highly controversial. Assessments of practical and investigative work in science, for example, increasingly a feature of British science education, would be inappropriate in a different educational system where most teaching was through books and academic exercises. Some comparisons have been made that show how in mathematics and some aspects of science, British pupils do not attain such high standards as their Japanese equivalents. A publication by the International Associates for the Evaluation of Educational Achievement, *Science Achievement in Seventeen Countries*, showed that this was particularly true in the initial stages of secondary education, where England is listed with Hong Kong, Italy, Singapore, and the USA. These are all countries which the report says should be concerned about 'the scientific literacy of their general workforce'. Finland, Hungary, Japan, and Sweden led the field in mass secondary science attainment. The same report, however, shows that at more advanced levels Hong Kong, England, and Singapore, together with Hungary and Japan would appear to be educating their élites well.

There arises from this a recurring message for schools. Traditionally, the higher-attaining pupils can hold their own with the best in the world. But as we move into the twenty-first century, these standards need deepening to cover a much wider range of pupils. The jobs of the twenty-first century will require much higher levels of skill and knowledge than those of the twentieth. In recent years national tests show significant improvement but the key issue is not whether standards are falling, but whether they are rising fast enough. A great deal of evidence suggests the rather common-sense idea that people respond to the expectations you have of them. In school this is especially true. The National Curriculum defines what the vast majority of pupils should know at certain ages and, over time, this could contribute significantly to raising standards.

Improving communication

Creating a curriculum entitlement and raising standards are the two major justifications for a prescribed National Curriculum. There are, however, further supporting arguments. Many parents in the past found the curriculum a rather obscure part of the school's activities. There is research evidence and, again, a good deal of common-sense support for the view that the more parents know about what their children are expected to learn and achieve, the more likely the children are to succeed. Information such as this has been difficult for parents to obtain, not because of any obstruction on the part of teachers, but because there was no common language or agreed structure within which to explain or report on children's progress. Even where examination syllabuses existed, for GCSE or A level, for example, parents could find it difficult to ascertain even roughly what point in the syllabus their child had reached. In many instances pupils would sit the examination without ever having seen the syllabus. The National Curriculum, with its relatively straightforward terminology, provides the basis for greater clarity in school–parent communication.

Progress and continuity

The National Curriculum is an important means of improving the links between primary and secondary schools. Despite the existence of many well-organized liaison schemes, there has been much concern about the problems of transfer from primary to secondary schools. Secondary teachers receiving pupils from different primary schools have found it difficult to establish the subject-content previously covered, or the level of attainment reached by individual children. It has not been unusual for secondary teachers to talk about 'starting from scratch'. This was particularly problematic in subjects where knowledge tends to build up sequentially, for example, in mathematics, science, and perhaps music. The National Curriculum provides a focus for better record-keeping and monitoring of progress between teachers and between schools.

All these arguments apply equally where forms of schooling other than primary and secondary exist. In some areas, the existence of middle schools, or junior high schools, means that children have two changes of school, rather than the more usual one. Many families have to move from place to place because of job opportunities. Even within the same school, teachers move to new posts, fall ill, or are involved in in-service training. These events can lead to significant breaks in the continuity of children's education. Again, the National Curriculum is a means of minimizing disruption.

Individual attainment

Finally, there is one major potential advantage of the National Curriculum that could radically change the way schooldays are experienced. Many parents will remember the monthly or termly 'position in class' lists compiled by form teachers. Similar lists were drawn up to describe the end-of-term examination results. Grading schemes might also have been used; in many schools A–E for attainment and 1–5 for effort were widely adopted in the 1970s and 1980s. Most of these schemes involved ranking pupils one against another, and in fact throughout the twentieth century this has been the major form of assessment in British schools. Inevitably, a large proportion of pupils came out as below average.

Rank order is most significant when it determines access to limited places, for example, at universities. The public examination system served this purpose for most of this century. The 11-plus examination, which selected about 20 per cent of the age group to go on to a grammar school education, is one of the best-known examples of rank ordering. The statistical model upon which the tests

and examinations were based was the bell curve, with the bulk of the
population (average performance) found at the top of the curve, and
the most or least able on the extremities (see Figure 1).

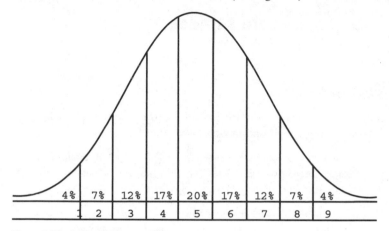

4%	7%	12%	17%	20%	17%	12%	7%	4%
1	2	3	4	5	6	7	8	9

Figure 1: The bell curve chart

Many of those who have advocated a National Curriculum argue
that we should be moving away from standards based on relative
information (how one pupil compares with others) to absolute
standards (whether a pupil has shown individual knowledge and
competency in the different parts of the curriculum). Everyone
should be able to achieve the higher levels of attainment, it is argued.
A Government-appointed Task Group, set up to work out how the
National Curriculum should be assessed, said that any system should
be confined to 'the assessment of "performance" or "attainment"', and
they were not recommending any attempt to assess separately the
problematic notion of underlying 'ability'.

This represents something of a challenge for school organizations
where ranking still lives on. For the most part the 'position in class'
lists have disappeared, but in teachers' and parents' minds the old idea,
discredited by many of the developments in psychology, that children
are born with a fixed potential, remains. The National Curriculum
provides a national yardstick against which unrecognized potential
can be realized and acknowledged.

The core subjects

English

The National Curriculum for English begins with the following
statement about the importance of the subject:

> *English is a vital way of communicating in school, in public life and*
> *internationally. Literature in English is rich and influential, reflecting*
> *the experience of people from many countries and times.*
>
> *In studying English, pupils develop skills in speaking, listening and*
> *writing. It enables them to express themselves creatively and*
> *imaginatively and to communicate with others effectively. Pupils learn*
> *to become enthusiastic and critical readers of stories, poetry and drama*
> *as well as non-fiction and media texts. The study of English helps*
> *pupils understand how language works by looking at its patterns,*
> *structures and origins. Using this knowledge pupils can choose and*
> *adapt what they say and write in different situations.*

How English is taught has been a subject of much debate. In the
development of the National Curriculum, the value placed on
different aspects of teaching was often controversial. The working
party that produced the first draft of a National Curriculum for
English outlined a number of models of English teaching:

■ a view that English is about *personal growth*; an individual and
creative engagement with literature, particularly, was stressed

■ a view that saw the potential of English as a *cross-curricular*
vehicle for learning, servicing other subject domains

■ a view that stressed the *adult, vocational needs* of pupils, in terms
of communication skills, especially

■   a view that the *cultural heritage* of the nation is nurtured by study of those notable texts which have been generally agreed to contribute to it

■   a view that work in English could contribute to a critical *cultural analysis* of the world in which pupils live.

Different teachers may emphasise one view rather than another, or different combinations of these views. These may only be implicit in their practice or explicit reference may be made in school policy documents. The National Curriculum for English contains elements of all of these views.

The attainment targets and programmes of study in English

The programmes of study are organised into three main areas, or attainment targets (ATs):

Speaking and listening (AT1)

Reading (AT2)

Writing (AT3).

Each of these areas of the curriculum specifies a range of knowledge, skills and understanding to be addressed. However, it is stressed that each area must be approached within an integrated programme of work which allows strong links between them. So, where a teacher chooses to highlight skills related to report writing, for example, it is expected that speaking and listening as well as reading, will feature within the plans for classwork and related homework. The programmes of study set out a series of general statements of what pupils will learn in English in each of the four key stages. These are:

Key stage 1:

In English, during key stage 1 pupils learn to speak confidently and listen to what others have to say. They begin to read and write independently and with enthusiasm. They use language to explore their own experiences and imaginary worlds.

Key stage 2:

In English, during key stage 2 pupils learn to change the way they speak and write to suit different situations, purposes and audiences. They read a range of texts and respond to different layers of meaning in them. They explore the use of language in literary and non-literary texts and learn how language works.

Key stage 3:

In English, during key stage 3 pupils develop confidence in speaking and writing for public and formal purposes. They also develop their ability to evaluate the way language is used. They read classic and contemporary texts and explore social and moral issues.

Key stage 4:

In English, during key stage 4 pupils learn to use language confidently, both in their academic studies and for the world beyond school. They use and analyse complex features of language. They are keen readers who can read many kinds of text and make articulate and perceptive comments about them.

It is expected that each key stage builds upon what is known about and able to be done by pupils in earlier phases of development. The programmes of study for speaking and listening in key stage 1, for example, build upon pupils' early language developments as well as on pupils' prior experience of using language to imagine and recreate roles and experiences, attentive listening and response, and interacting with others in play and to get things done. By key stage 4, it is assumed that sufficient work has been done and expertise developed by pupils during key stage 3 in the use of speaking and writing for public and formal purposes. The key stage 4 programme of study builds on this development *in order that* confident articulation of thought can be made for what the National Curriculum refers to as *the world beyond school.*

In addition to these general statements, the programmes of study outline in some detail the knowledge, skills and understanding requiring development in the three attainment targets across the key stages.

So, at **key stage 1** the programme of study for attainment target 1 (speaking and listening) addresses the organisation of thought in *speaking*, sustaining concentration and commenting relevantly while *listening*, interacting productively as a *group discussant*, participating in a range of *drama activities* and making appropriate responses. An introduction to the main features of *standard English* and to *language variation* is a requirement too.

Breadth of study – key stage 1

A key element of the programmes of study, and uniting all the key stages is the breadth of study that it is expected should be provided. Clear expectations for planning and for teaching and learning are... relating expressly to an idea of entitlement for all children to wide and productive study. These entitlement elements in key stage 1, for example, are:

Speaking

The range should include:

(a) telling stories, real and imagined

(b) reading aloud and reciting

(c) describing events and experiences

(d) speaking to different people, including friends, the class, teachers and other adults.

Listening

The range should include opportunities for pupils to listen to:

(a) each other

(b) adults giving detailed explanations and presentations (for example, describing how a model works, reading aloud)

(c)   recordings (for example, radio, television).

Group discussion and interaction

The range of purposes should include:

(a)   making plans and investigating

(b)   sharing ideas and experiences

(c)   commenting and reporting.

Drama activities

The range should include:

(a)   working in role

(b)   presenting drama and stories to others (for example, telling a story through tableaux or using a narrator)

(c)   responding to performances.

This *breadth of study* duty and the implications for teaching and learning attached to it, can usefully be illustrated through the requirements for reading across key stages 2, 3 and 4.

Breadth of study in key stages 2, 3 and 4: reading

Key stage 2: reading

Literature

The range should include:

(a)   a range of modern fiction by significant children's authors

(b)   long-established children's fiction

(c)   a range of good-quality modern poetry

(d)   classic poetry

(e)   texts drawn from a variety of cultures and traditions

(f)   myths, legends and traditional stories

(g)   playscripts.

Non-fiction and non-literary texts

The range should include:

(a)   diaries, autobiographies, biographies, letters

(b)   print and ICT-based reference and information materials (for example, textbooks, reports, encyclopaedias, handbooks, dictionaries, thesauruses, glossaries, CD-ROMs, internet)

(c)   newspapers, magazines, articles, leaflets, brochures, advertisements.

The breadth of study requirements for key stages 3 and 4 build upon this, with an element of teacher choice indicated at these levels.

Key stages 3 and 4: reading

Literature – the range should include:

(a)   *plays, novels, short stories and poetry from the English literary heritage,* including:

    (i)   *two plays by Shakespeare*
       one of which should be studied in key stage 3

    (ii)   *drama by major playwrights*
       (examples of major playwrights –
       William Congreve, Oliver Goldsmith, Christopher Marlowe, Sean O'Casey, Harold Pinter, J B Priestley, Peter Shaffer, G B Shaw, R B Sheridan, Oscar Wilde)

    (iii)   *works of fiction by two major writers published before 1914*
       selected from the following list – Jane Austen, Charlotte Bronte, Emily Bronte, John Bunyan, Wilkie Collins, Joseph Conrad, Daniel Defoe, Charles Dickens, Arthur Conan Doyle, George Eliot, Henry Fielding, Elizabeth Gaskell, Thomas Hardy, Henry James, Mary Shelley, Robert Louis Stevenson, Jonathan Swift, Anthony Trollope, H G Wells

    (iv)   *two works of fiction by major writers published after 1914*
       (examples of fiction by major writers after 1914 –
       E M Forster, William Golding, Graham Greene,

Aldous Huxley, James Joyce, D H Lawrence, Katherine
Mansfield, George Orwell, Muriel Spark, William Trevor,
Evelyn Waugh)

(v) *poetry by four major poets published before 1914*
selected from the following list – Matthew Arnold,
Elizabeth Barrett Browning, William Blake, Emily Bronte,
Robert Browning, Robert Burns, Lord Byron, Geoffrey
Chaucer,   John Clare, Samuel Taylor Coleridge, John
Donne, John Dryden, Thomas Gray, George Herbert,
Robert Herrick, Gerard Manley Hopkins, John Keats,
Andrew Marvell, John Milton, Alexander Pope, Christina
Rossetti, William Shakespeare (sonnets), Percy Bysshe
Shelley, Edmund Spenser, Alfred Lord Tennyson, Henry
Vaughan, William Wordsworth, Sir Thomas Wyatt

(vi) *poetry by four major poets published after 1914*
(examples of major poets after 1914 –
W H Auden, Gilliam Clarke, Keith Douglas, T S Eliot,
U A Fanthorpe, Thomas Hardy, Seamus Heaney, Ted
Hughes, Elizabeth Jennings, Philip Larkin, Wilfred Owen,
Sylvia Plath, Stevie Smith, Edward Thomas, R S Thomas,
W B Yeats)

(b)   *recent and contemporary drama, fiction and poetry written for young*
people and adults
(examples of recent and contemporary drama, fiction and
poetry –
Drama: Alan Ayckbourn, Samuel Beckett, Alan Bennett,
Robert Bolt, Brian Friel, Willis Hall, David Hare, Willie
Russell, R C Sherriff, Arnold Wesker
Fiction: J G Ballard, Berlie Doherty, Susan Hill, Laurie Lee,
Joan Lingard, Bill Naughton, Alan Sillitoe, Mildred Taylor,
Robert Westall
Poetry: Simon Armitage, James Berry, Douglas Dunn, Liz
Lochhead, Adrian Mitchell, Edwin Muir, Grace Nichols, Jo
Shapcott)

(c)   *drama, fiction and poetry by major writers from different cultures and*
traditions
(examples of drama, fiction and poetry by major writers from

different cultures and traditions –
Drama: Athol Fugard, Arthur Miller, Wole Soyinka, Tennessee Williams
Fiction: Chinua Achebe, Maya Angelou, Willa Cather, Anita Desai, Nadine Gordimer, Ernest Hemingway, H H Richardson, Doris Lessing, R K Narayan, John Steinbeck, Ngug wa Thing'o
Poetry: E K Brathwaite, Emily Dickinson, Robert Frost, Robert Lowell, Les Murray, Rabindranath Tagore, Derek Walcott)

(d) *Non-fiction and non-literary texts*
The range should include:
(i) literary non-fiction
(ii) print and ICT-based information and reference texts
(iii) media and moving image texts (for example, newspapers, magazines, advertisements, television, films, videos).
(Examples of *non-fiction and non-literary texts*
Personal record and viewpoints on society: Peter Ackroyd, James Baldwin, John Berger, James Boswell, Vera Brittain, Lord Byron, William Cobbett, Gerald Durrell, Robert Graves, Samuel Johnson, Laurie Lee, Samuel Pepys, Flora Thompson, Beatrice Webb, Dorothy Wordsworth
Travel writing: Jan Morris, Freya Stark, Laurens Van der Post
Reportage: James Cameron, Winston Churchill, Alistair Cooke, Dilys Powell.
The natural world: David Attenborough, Rachel Carson, Charles Darwin)

The authors indicated in brackets are non-statutory, offered as ideas-for-consideration. There is a proviso, however, that a specified number of writers must be chosen from each of the categories, so as to ensure **breadth of study**. Such an approach does, nevertheless, imply the idea of an 'approved' canon of texts and writers. Vigorous debate has arisen in relation to such a canon, not least in relation to those writers absent, as well as present, in such lists.

Breadth of study: assessment across the key stages

It will be useful here to look at the issue of assessment in relation to the third attainment target, *writing* (AT3). *What* is assessed routinely in English is closely linked to course and syllabus requirements. These in turn are determined by the National Curriculum programmes of study, together with the examination boards' papers for 16+ pupils at the end of key stage 4. The standard assessment tasks (SATs), at the end of the key stages 1, 2 and 3 programmes of study are similarly fashioned. Level descriptors are given for each of the three attainment targets. These provide performance outcomes expected for a particular age group (key stage) in relation to speaking and listening, reading and writing, shaped by the breadth of study requirements.

So, at **key stage 1**, the 'breadth' to be assessed in relation to writing requires tasks that 'address the following ranges of purposes, readers and forms of writing':

The *range of purposes* for writing should include these:

(a)   to communicate to others

(b)   to create imaginary worlds

(c)   to explore experience

(d)   to organise and explain information.

Pupils should be taught the value of writing for remembering and developing ideas.

The *range of readers* for writing should include teachers, other adults, children and the writers themselves.

The *range of forms* of writing should include narratives, poems, notes, lists, captions, records, messages, and instructions.

At the end of key stage 2

The *range of purposes* for writing should include these:

(a)   to imagine and explore feelings and ideas, focussing on creative uses of language and how to interest the reader

(b) to inform and explain, focussing on the subject matter and how to convey it in sufficient detail for the reader

(c) to persuade, focussing on how arguments and evidence are built up and the language used to convince the reader

(d) to review and comment on what has been read, seen or heard, focussing on both the topic and the writer's view of it.

Pupils should also:

Be taught to use writing to help their thinking, investigating, organising and learning.

The *range of readers* for writing should include teachers, the class, other children, adults, the wider community and imagined readers.

The range of forms of writing should include narratives, poems, playscripts, reports, explanations, opinions, instructions, reviews, commentaries.

By the end of key stage 4 pupils should have been taught the appropriate knowledge, skills and understanding through addressing the following range of purposes, readers and forms of writing.

The *range of purposes* for writing should include these:

(a) to imagine, explore and entertain, focussing on creative, aesthetic and literary uses of language. The forms for such writing should be drawn from different kinds of stories, poems, playscripts, autobiographies, screenplays, diaries

(b) to inform, explain and describe, focussing on conveying information and ideas clearly. The forms for such writing should be drawn from memos, minutes, accounts, information leaflets, prospectuses, plans, records, summaries

(c) to persuade, argue and advise, focussing on presenting a case and influencing the reader. The forms for such writing should be drawn from brochures, advertisements, editorials, articles and letters conveying opinions, campaign literature, polemical essays

(d)   to analyse, review and comment, focussing on considered and evaluative views of ideas, texts and issues. The forms for such writing should be drawn from reviews, commentaries, articles, essays, reports.

Pupils should also be taught to use writing for thinking and learning (for example, for hypothesising, paraphrasing, summarising, noting).

The *range of readers* for writing should include specific, known readers, a large, unknown readership and the pupils themselves.

At the end of key stage 1 teacher assessment takes precedence. Assessment tasks align closely with the programmes of study and the requirements about breadth. **At the end of key stages 2 and 3**, equal weighting is statutorily given to public test results and teacher assessment. In practice, however, the public reporting of test results (which do not include teacher assessments), together with the publicly declared national targets set for 2002 in English, undermine the stated policy somewhat. **At the end of key stage 4**, English examination results in their entirety are in the public domain. These are frequently the subject of national debates, particularly in relation to definitions about 'standards' of literacy as well as to implications of league tables of results for teachers, schools, and local authorities.

Examples of writing tasks required at two of the key testing points follow (Figures 1-3).

The first is taken from the standard assessment task (SAT) for writing (AT3) at key stage 1 for the year 2000. At key stage 1, pupils are strongly supported in their writing in terms of introductory discussion, ideas-sharing and talking and looking at books. For this task, the teacher reads a story, Fly By Night. Pupils are then required to write a letter from Blink, the baby owl in this story, describing his flight. A structured planning sheet such as the one shown in Figure 1 is given to pupils to help them prepare for the task. It is intended that the quality of the writing itself will be assessed. Barriers to this – such as pupils not understanding the task, or not remembering key ideas discussed – should not have an over-weighted effect on what can be written.

Planning your writing

Make a note of your ideas here to help you remember them.

Letter from Blink

Who is Blink writing his letter to?

[ ]

Write down some of the things Blink saw on his flight.

[ ]　　　　[ ]

[ ]　　　　[ ]

Write down some interesting words to describe what Blink saw and how he felt when he was flying.

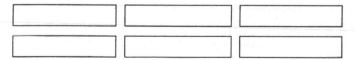

[ ]　　[ ]　　[ ]

[ ]　　[ ]　　[ ]

Think about

- how to start your letter

- how to organise your ideas

- how to end your letter

Figure 1

Performance outcomes are provided by the level descriptions. At key stage 1 the expected level for this age-group is level 2, sub-divided into 2A (the highest at this level), 2B and 2C.

A pupil's response to a similar key stage 1 SATs task is shown below in Figure 2. Emily has developed a story about an argument over a chocolate bar in response to the book, *Jamaica and Brianna*. As a piece of writing this was assessed as level 2B.

Emily

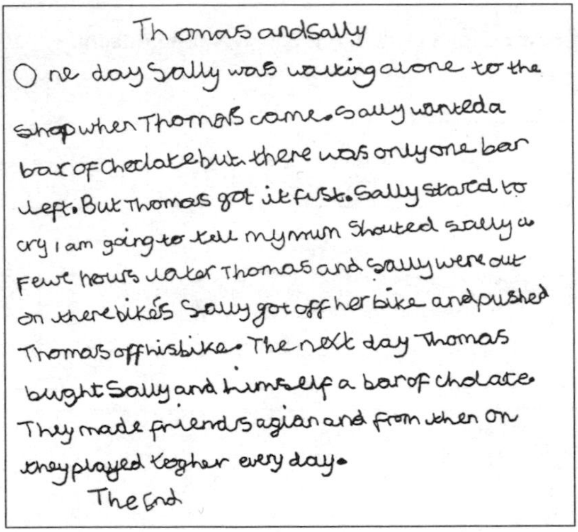
Thomas andSally
One day Sally was walking alone to the
shop when Thomas came. Sally wanted a
bar of chcolate but there was only one bar
left. But Thomas got it first. Sally stared to
cry I am going to tell my mum Shouted sally a
Fewe hours later Thomas and sally were out
on there bikes Sally got off her bike and pushed
Thomas off his bike. The next day Thomas
bught Sally and himself a bar of cholate.
They made friends agian and from then on
they played togher every day.
The End

Emily wrote in response to *Jamaica and Brianna*, adapting the central event of the book by developing a story about children falling out over a chocolate bar. The situation is quickly described, 'Sally wanted a bar of chocolate but there was only one bar left,' and the consequent events are rapidly introduced. The story has a good pace, the plot is well structured and some sentences are extended and varied. There is also clear characterisation, although the characters' motivation is taken to be self-evident and no explanation is provided for Thomas' change of heart. Simple sentence punctuation is accurate, and where words are misspelt there is a clear attempt to recall a visual pattern or letter string, eg 'bught', 'agian'. Emily's handwriting is joined and reasonably clear.

This piece of writing was assessed as level 2B.

Figure 2

At **key stage 3**, those pupils judged to be levels 1–3 in English are teacher-assessed only. In 2000 two test papers were used to assess pupils at levels 4–7. An extension paper determined those pupils achieving levels 8–10. For levels 4–7, the first paper comprised an essay and comprehension; the second a Shakespeare paper. The extract given below in Figure 3 illustrates one of the questions from the Shakespeare paper about Act 2 Scene 5 from *Twelfth Night*. This is one of two scenes prescribed for detailed study. The marking scheme for this question makes it clear that attention to performance and a clear knowledge and understanding of the text of the scene will both be assessed.

Twelfth Night

Act 2 Scene 5

TASK 6

In this scene, Sir Toby and Sir Andrew are involved in playing a humorous trick on Malvolio.

Imagine you are going to direct this scene for a class performance.

What advice would you give to your actors to make this scene funny for the audience?

Before you begin to write you should decide:

- how you want the actors on stage at the beginning of the scene to prepare for Malvolio's entrance;

- how you want the actor playing Malvolio to speak and behave during the scene;

- how you want the actors playing Sir Toby and Sir Andrew to add to the humour through their reactions to Malvolio throughout the scene.

Read the task again before you begin to write your answer.

Twelfth Night

Figure 3

The assessment arrangements for **key stage 4** now stipulate that a maximum of 30% is available for a coursework element. Animated campaigns to maintain 100% coursework literature and language options on the grounds of pupil motivation and teacher autonomy so as to preserve, ironically, breadth of study, have in effect been rejected. The different examination boards for English offer examination papers with slightly varied components, whilst meeting the National Curriculum requirements for the subject.

Drama and media texts in English at key stages 3 and 4

The requirements for *drama in English* can be seen as an extension of the breadth of study outlined for the speaking and listening programme of study and the attainment targets attached to it. In key stages 3 and 4, pupils must be encouraged to participate in a range of drama activities and to evaluate their own and others' contributions, and should be taught to:

(a)   use a variety of dramatic techniques to explore ideas, issues, texts and meanings

(b)   use different ways to convey action, character, atmosphere and tension when they are scripting and performing in plays (for example, through dialogue, movement, pace)

(c)   appreciate how the structure and organisation of scenes and plays contribute to dramatic effect

(d)   evaluate critically performances of dramas that they have watched or in which they have taken part.

And in terms of: *media and moving image texts at key stages 3 and 4:*

Pupils should be taught:

(a)   how meaning is conveyed in texts that include print, images and sometimes sounds

(b)   how choice of form, layout and presentation contribute to effect (for example, font, caption, illustration in printed text, sequencing, framing, soundtrack in moving image text)

(c)   how the nature and purpose of media products influence content and meaning (for example, selection of stories for a front page or news broadcast)

(d)   how audiences and readers choose and respond to media.

English and other curriculum subjects

The revised National Curriculum is much more explicit about how all subject teachers might contribute to pupils' ability to use language in different contexts. The requirement is placed upon every subject area to contribute to the development of pupils' skills to:

■   express themselves correctly and appropriately and to read accurately and with understanding. Since standard English, spoken and written, is the predominant language in which knowledge and skills are taught and learned, pupils should be taught to recognise and use standard English;

■   use correct spelling and punctuation and follow grammatical conventions; to organise writing in logical and coherent forms;

■   use language precisely and cogently in speaking;

■   listen effectively, responding constructively

■   read with understanding, to locate and use information; to follow a process or argument, to synthesise and adapt what they learn from their reading;

■   know the specialist vocabulary of subjects and how to spell these words; to use the patterns of language necessary and commonly used for individual subjects.

The National Literacy Strategy

The National Literacy Strategy (NLS) was implemented in key stages 1 and 2, following the report of a Literacy Task Force in 1997. A national target for literacy was set, linked to the attainment levels of the National Curriculum for English: by 2002, 80% of 11-year-olds will be expected to reach level 4 or above in the key stage 2 English tests (a satisfactory attainment for key stage 1 is set at level 2).

A daily Literacy Hour is now a statutory requirement in primary schools, focussing on regular word, sentence and text-level activities (see Chapter 5). This work is now being strengthened in the secondary sector which is seeking to embed in a practical fashion the guiding principle articulated in the *Implementation of the National Literacy Strategy* document:

> *Every secondary school should specialise in literacy and set targets for improvements in English. Similarly, every teacher should contribute to promoting it… In shaping their plans it is essential that secondary schools do not see work on reading and writing as exclusively the province of a few teachers in the English and learning support departments.*

Mathematics

The National Curriculum for mathematics begins with the following statement about the importance of the subject:

> *Mathematics equips pupils with a uniquely powerful set of tools to understand and change the world. These tools include logical reasoning, problem-solving skills, and the ability to think in abstract ways. Mathematics is important in everyday life, many forms of employment, science and technology, medicine, the economy, the environment and development, and in public decision-making. Different cultures have contributed to the development and application of mathematics. Today, the subject transcends cultural boundaries and its importance is universally recognised. Mathematics is a creative discipline. It can stimulate moments of pleasure and wonder when a pupil solves a problem for the first time, discovers a more elegant solution to that problem, or suddenly sees hidden connections.*

The idea that mathematics can be seen as a creative discipline, stimulating pleasure and wonder through active engagement in discovery, exploration and problem-solving is familiar to those who see themselves as successful mathematicians. To many people, however, it may seem far removed from their own memories of the subject.

The challenge for the designers of the National Curriculum, and for mathematics teachers, is to ensure that the core knowledge, skills and understanding of mathematics are taught in a way that builds confidence and a real interest in the subject. Pupils need to be able to move beyond predictable, repetitive series of exercises (which have a place in building skills) to be able to address unfamiliar and sometimes complex problems. Real world situations are rarely predictable and mathematics, therefore, always represents something of an investigation into the world around us. In mathematics education, the phrase 'the investigative approach' is often used to describe the newer approaches to the subject that go beyond mere role skill acquisition.

The National Curriculum for mathematics includes the content expected of a mathematics curriculum but it is underpinned by the belief that the aim for pupils is that they become confident problem-solvers, even explorers within mathematics.

As well as the National Curriculum for mathematics, there is also a National Numeracy Strategy Framework for teaching mathematics from reception to year 6 (DfEE, 1999) and it is useful to understand how the two fit together. The National Curriculum describes what must be taught in each key stage whilst the Framework provides guidance to supplement the order. Each is compatible with the other so that fully implementing the Numeracy Framework will fulfil the statutory duty in relation to the National Curriculum. The Numeracy Framework contains a set of yearly teaching programmes, illustrating how mathematics can be planned and taught at key stages 1 and 2. Thus the National Curriculum specifies what is to be taught, the Framework relates to ways of planning and teaching it.

As well has having a Numeracy Strategy for key stages 1 and 2, there is now a Numeracy Strategy for key stage 3 which proposes specific teaching strategies and programmes for years 7, 8 and 9. Again, this is compatible with the National Curriculum.

The programmes of study

The programmes of study specify the 'knowledge, skills and understanding' in which pupils make progress in each key stage. There is also a requirement that within each key stage, teaching strategies reflect the overall need of being able to use and apply the mathematics learnt.

The knowledge, skills and understanding in the programmes of study are in:

Key stage 1	Key stage 2	Key stages 3 and 4
■ number	■ number	■ number and algebra
■ shape, space and measures	■ shape, space and measures	■ shape, space and measures
	■ handling data	■ handling data

These sections are not taught in isolation from each other. In fact, it is expected that where ideas link across number and algebra; shape, space and measures; and handling data, those connections should be made explicit to help pupil learning.

There are two programmes of study at key stage 4 – foundation and higher. Pupils are taught one or the other depending on the level they have reached by the end of key stage 3. The higher programme of study is designed for pupils who have confidently attained a level 5 or above at the end of key stage 3.

Attainment targets and level descriptions

The attainment targets for mathematics set out what knowledge, skills and understanding pupils of different abilities and maturities are expected to have by the end of each key stage. There are eight level descriptions of increasing difficulty, together with a description for 'exceptional performance' above level eight for each of the following four attainment targets.

- using and applying mathematics;
- number and algebra;
- shape, space and measures;
- handling data.

Examples from the programmes of study and level descriptions

At key stage 2

Pupils are to be taught through activities which help them to *think* mathematically. These include approximating and estimating, using patterns and relationships to explore simple algebraic ideas, applying skills in a range of contexts, drawing inferences from data, using a variety of resources and materials, making decisions about appropriate use of calculators.

Within shape, space and measures, the programme of study identifies four strands to be addressed within the key stage: using and applying shape, space and measures; understanding properties of shape; understanding properties of position and movement; understanding measures.

- The first strand of using and applying shape, space and measures includes attention to:

Problem solving – e.g. approach spatial problems flexibly, including trying alternative approaches to overcome difficulties;

Communicating – e.g. use geometrical notation and symbols correctly;

Reasoning – use mathematical reasoning to explain features of shape and space.

- The second strand of understanding properties of shape expects pupils to be taught (for example) to:

Make and draw with increasing accuracy 2-D and 3-D shapes and patterns; recognise reflective symmetry in regular polygons; recognise their geometrical features and properties including angles, faces, pairs of parallel lines and symmetry, and use these to classify shapes and solve problems.

■ The third strand of understanding properties of position and movement expects pupils to be taught (for example) to:

Transform objects in practical situations; transform images using ICT; visualise and predict the position of a shape following a rotation, reflection or translation.

■ The fourth strand of understanding measures expects pupils to be taught (for example) to:

Read the time from analogue and digital 12- and 24-hour clocks; use units of time – seconds, minutes, hours, days, weeks – and know the relationship between them.

It is expected that the majority of pupils by the end of key stage 2 will have reached level 4, and the level description for this in relation to attainment target 3, shape, space and measure, is:

Pupils make 3-D models by linking given faces or edges, draw common 2-D shapes in different orientations on grids. They reflect simple shapes in a mirror line. They choose and use appropriate units and instruments, interpreting, with appropriate accuracy, numbers on a range of measuring instruments. They find the perimeters of simple shapes and find areas by counting squares.

At key stage 4, higher

Examples here have been chosen again within shape, space and measures to help identify the progression between key stages.

Pupils should be familiar and confident using standard procedures but they should also be given opportunities to explore and solve unfamiliar problems in a range of contexts. They should engage in activities in which they progress towards understanding and formulating proofs in algebra and geometry. They should also be choosing for themselves appropriate ICT tools for solving problems, representing and manipulating geometrical shapes, and presenting and analysing data.

The programme of study identifies four strands to be addressed within the key stage at this higher level:

■   using and applying shape, space and measures, with attention to:

    (a) *problem solving*, for example:

        select the problem-solving strategies to use in geometrical work, and consider and explain the extent to which the selections made were appropriate

    (b) *communicating*, for example:

        communicate mathematically, with emphasis on a critical examination of the presentation and organisation of results, and on effective use of symbols and geometrical diagrams

    (c) *reasoning*, for example:

        show step-by-step deduction in solving a geometrical problem

■   geometrical reasoning, attending to: properties of angles and other rectilinear shapes; and properties of circles

■   transformations and co-ordinates, attending to: specifying transformations; properties of transformations; co-ordinates; and vectors

■   measures and construction, attending to: measure; construction; mensuration and loci.

Assessment at the end of key stage 4 is through national qualifications. However, it is useful to look at the level description for level 8 (which is more demanding than the relevant criteria associated with a grade C in GCSE) in shape, space and measure:

> *Pupils understand and use congruence and mathematical similarity. They use sine, cosine and tangent in right-angled triangles when solving problems in two dimensions. They distinguish between formulae for perimeter, area and volume by considering dimensions.*

Assessment

The programmes of study set out a whole range of skills, knowledge and understanding. Designing an assessment system that fairly measures attainment across all the activities is a challenge. Timed written tests, for example, may not be able to measure achievements in, for example, choosing and using a variety of ICT tools or tackling unfamiliar mathematics problems in different contexts. The challenge for teachers is to ensure good understanding of the areas to be covered by tests as well as the wider curriculum illustrated by the statement of the importance of mathematics at the beginning of this section.

The pattern at key stage 3 is that there are two written papers (one which is non-calculator and one in which the use of a calculator is allowed) and a mental arithmetic test. The written papers are tiered, which means that pupils take different papers depending on their anticipated level of achievement. Thus, there are papers covering work at levels 3–5; 4–6; 5–7; 6–8. There is a further extension paper to assess pupils working at a level of 'exceptional performance'.

Examples of questions from the mathematics tests covering levels 4–6 and 5–7 set for key stage 3 (where it is expected that the majority of pupils will have reached level 5/6 by the end of the key stage) are on the following two pages.

Figure 1: 1999, key stage 3, tier 4–6, paper 1 calculator not allowed, question 9 (same as question 5 on tier 5–7 paper)

9.

Symmetry

An equilateral triangle has **3 lines of symmetry**.

It has **rotational symmetry** of **order 3**

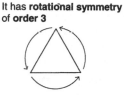

Write the letter of each shape in the correct space in the table below.
You may use a mirror or tracing paper to help you.
The letters for the first two shapes have been written for you.

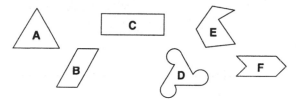

Number of Lines of Symmetry

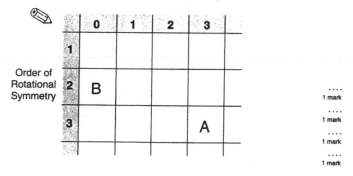

	0	1	2	3
1				
2	B			
3				A

Order of Rotational Symmetry

. . . .
1 mark
. . . .
1 mark
. . . .
1 mark
. . . .
1 mark

Figure 2: 1999, key stage 3, tier 4–6, paper 2 calculator allowed, question 11 (same as question 7 on tier 5–7 paper)

11.

(a) A circle has a radius of 15cm.

Calculate the **area** of the circle.
Show your working.

15cm

Circles

....
....
2 marks

.... cm²

(b) A different circle has a **circumference** of **120cm**.

What is the **radius** of the circle?
Show your working.

....
....
2 marks

.... cm

Science

Why should science be a part of the National Curriculum? Society needs scientists but only a minority of pupils go on to study science after GCSE. Even fewer become what we would call 'scientists'. For the majority of pupils, studying science needs to be justified on broader grounds.

Today, science is an increasingly important and prominent part of our lives. Through the media we are bombarded with issues that require scientific understanding. Climate change, cloning, nuclear power, or DNA fingerprinting are all major areas of public concern. Taking part in the moral and ethical debates surrounding such issues requires a population that is scientifically literate. On a personal level, understanding science enables people to evaluate evidence and make their own decisions. Current concerns, for example, include the risks of using mobile phones, vaccinating babies, or eating genetically modified foods. Although few students may become 'scientists', scientific knowledge can be of value in a wide range of vocational contexts, from hairdressing to engineering. Finally, science is one of the greatest achievements of human culture; a study of evolution or the origins of the universe has a profound contribution to make to an understanding of what it is to be human.

The importance of science is highlighted in the science National Curriculum document:

> *Science stimulates and excites pupils' curiosity about phenomena and events in the world around them. It also satisfies this curiosity with knowledge. Because science links direct practical experience with ideas, it can engage learners on many levels. Scientific method is about developing and evaluating explanations through experimental evidence and modelling. This is a spur to critical and creative thought. Through science, pupils understand how major scientific ideas contribute to technological change – impacting on industry, business and medicine and improving quality of life. Pupils recognise the cultural significance of science and trace its worldwide development. They learn to question and discuss science-based issues that may affect their own lives, the direction of society and the future of the world.*

It is, therefore, important that all pupils receive an education in science. If any pupils are denied access to science education, they are disenfranchised from a significant part of our culture and society.

Structure and organisation of the science curriculum

The scientific knowledge, skills and understanding to be taught are set out in four sections of the programmes of study for each key stage:

- ■ Sc1 Scientific enquiry
- ■ Sc2 Life processes and living things
- ■ Sc3 Materials and their properties
- ■ Sc4 Physical processes

Each of these sections consists of a number of different areas of study which are developed through each key stage. These areas are summarised below.

Areas of study in the programmes of study

Sc1: Scientific enquiry	Sc2: Life processes and living things	Sc3: Materials and their properties	Sc4: Physical processes
ideas and evidence investigative skills: ■ planning ■ obtaining evidence ■ presenting evidence (not key stage 1)	life processes cells and cell function (not key stage 1) humans and other animals green plants variation and classification	grouping / classifying materials changing materials separating mixtures of particles (not key stage 1) changing materials (not key stages 1 and 2)	electricity forces and motion light and sound the earth and beyond (not key stage 1) energy resources and energy transfer (not key stages 1 and 2)

considering evidence (not key stage 1) evaluating (not key stage 1)	living things in their environment	patterns of behaviour (not key stages 1 and 2)	waves (key stage 4 only) radioactivity (key stage 4 only)

Sc1 Scientific enquiry

A major part of Sc1 is the development of pupils' investigative skills. Teaching should ensure that scientific enquiry is taught through contexts taken from across the science National Curriculum. Through investigative work, pupils can develop their understanding of the content of science as well as learn about the scientific method and the nature of evidence.

Sc2, Sc3 and Sc4 – the content of science

Sc2, Sc3 and Sc4 are often referred to as 'biology, chemistry and physics', although on closer inspection it can be seen that there is a broader range of content, including elements of astronomy, earth science and biotechnology. The science curriculum also provides opportunities for developing awareness of environmental issues, economic and industrial understanding, health education and citizenship, as well providing links to numeracy and literacy.

In the past, biology, chemistry and physics were treated as three separate subjects. For some years now, schools have generally combined the sciences into one curriculum subject on the timetable. At key stage 4, most pupils study 'double science', which leads to a double GCSE qualification. A minority of pupils, for example, those who have talents in the arts or foreign languages, may follow the single science curriculum. The single science curriculum has less content than the double version, but the time allocated to scientific enquiry is virtually the same in each syllabus.

Programmes of study for each key stage

As with other subjects, there is progression between each key stage and the next. A summary of the work done in each key stage is provided in the National Curriculum orders. The key points are summarised below. Progression is explored further in the section on assessment.

Summary of key stages

Key stage 1	Pupils observe, explore and ask questions about living things, materials and phenomena. They begin to collect evidence to help them answer questions and to link this to simple scientific ideas. They consider whether tests are fair. They use reference materials to find out more about scientific ideas and communicate them using scientific language, drawings, charts and tables.
Key stage 2	Pupils learn about a wider range of living things, materials and phenomena. They begin to make links between ideas, and to explain things using simple models and theories. They apply their knowledge and understanding of scientific ideas to familiar phenomena, everyday things and their personal health. They begin to think about the positive and negative effects of scientific and technological developments on the environment and in other contexts. They carry out more systematic investigations and use a range of reference sources. They communicate ideas using a wide range of scientific language, conventional diagrams, charts and graphs.
Key stage 3	Pupils make connections between different areas of science. They use scientific ideas and models to explain phenomena and events, and to understand a range of familiar applications of science. They think about the positive and negative effects of scientific and technological developments on the environment and in other contexts. They take account of other

	views and understand why opinions may differ. They do more quantitative investigative work. They evaluate their work and the strength of evidence collected. They select and use a wide range of reference sources. They communicate clearly what they did and its significance. They learn how scientists work together on scientific developments and about the importance of experimental evidence in supporting scientific ideas.
Key stage 4 **(double science)**	Pupils learn about a wider range of scientific ideas and consider them in greater depth. They explore how technological advances relate to the scientific ideas underpinning them. They consider the power and limitations of science in addressing industrial, ethical and environmental issues, and how different groups have different views about the role of science. When investigating, they do more quantitative work and evaluate more critically. They communicate their ideas clearly and concisely in a variety of ways. They see how new theories may be controversial and how social and cultural contexts may affect the extent to which theories are accepted.

Breadth of study

At the end of the programmes of study for each key stage there is a section called 'Breadth of study'. While the previous sections outline *what* has to be taught, this stipulates features of *how* it should be taught. It includes, for example, the requirement that pupils should be taught the specified knowledge, skills and understanding through a range of domestic, industrial and environmental contexts. They should consider and evaluate scientific and technological developments, including those related to the environment, personal health and quality of life, and those raising ethical issues. Through the science curriculum they should be taught aspects of communication (e.g. technical language) and health and safety (e.g. risk assessment).

Assessment

Attainment targets and level descriptions

The attainment targets for science set out the 'knowledge, skills and understanding pupils of different abilities and maturities are expected to have by the end of each key stage' (as defined by the Education Act 1996). There are four attainment targets, one relating to each of the four sections of the programmes of study.

Progression in Sc1

The levels in each attainment target show the progress pupils make in their learning. There are several aspects to progression through the levels (and hence the key stages). In Sc1 (scientific enquiry) pupils' progress is characterised by:

- increasing pupil independence in decision making;
- drawing on more complex scientific knowledge when predicting, hypothesising, and concluding;
- an increasing use of quantitative investigative methods;
- an increasing number of investigations where more than one variable is pertinent;
- an increasing reliability and accuracy of investigations, observations and measurements;
- an increasing use of more sophisticated equipment;
- more critical evaluation of investigative work and evidence.

So, for example, by the end of key stage 2, the level descriptions indicate that a pupil at level 4 will typically:

> '...decide on an appropriate approach to answer a question.'

> '...make a series of observations and measurements that are adequate for the task.'

> '...begin to relate their conclusions to... scientific knowledge and understanding.'

Building on this, by the end of key stage 3, a pupil at level 6 will typically:

> '...use scientific knowledge and understanding to identify an appropriate approach.'

> '...they make enough observations, comparisons and measurements for the task. They measure a variety of quantities with precision, using instruments with fine scale divisions.'

> '...draw conclusions that are consistent with the evidence and use scientific knowledge and understanding to explain them.

Progression in Sc2, Sc3 and Sc4

In the content-based programmes of study (Sc2, Sc3 and Sc4), progression is characterised by:

- an increase in the range of areas studied and the links made between them;
- explaining more complex phenomena using accepted scientific ideas, models and theories;
- moving from naming and describing objects, to explaining structure and functions;
- increasing use of formal and generalised ideas;
- a more quantitative and mathematical view of phenomena;
- increasing use of complex scientific language, notation and conventions;
- seeing science move from a school activity to an understanding of the nature and impact of scientific and technological activity beyond the classroom.

The following extracts from the level descriptions indicate that, for example, a key stage 2 pupil working at level 4 in the attainment targets will typically:

> '...recognise that feeding relationships exist between plants and animals in a habitat...'

> '...describe differences between properties of different

materials and explain how these differences are used to classify substances.'

'...describe and explain simple physical phenomena [how to connect a component in an electric circuit].'

At key stage 3, a pupil working at level 6 in the attainment targets will typically:

'...explain that the distribution and abundance of organisms in habitats are affected by environmental factors.'

'...describe differences between the arrangement and movement of particles in solids, liquids and gases.'

'...give explanations of phenomena in which a number of factors have to be considered [e.g. the relative brightness of planets and stars].'

Testing at the end of key stages

At the end of each of key stages 1, 2 and 3, pupils are awarded a level in science by their teacher. Teacher assessment is based on pupil performance in all four attainment targets over time. An important part of the teacher assessment is focused on pupils' practical and investigative work.

In addition to a teacher assessment, pupils at the end of key stages 2 and 3 are also assessed through formal, written tests in science. The tests are designed to assess pupils' knowledge and understanding of science across the whole of the programme of study. Each test contains questions related to Sc2, Sc3 and Sc4. Pupils' understanding of scientific enquiry (Sc1) is also partly assessed through the questions, as all are set in experimental and investigative contexts. The skills that can be assessed through the written tests include:

- understanding the use of evidence in science;
- planning how to investigate a scientific question;
- considering hazards and how to work safely;
- interpretation and evaluation of data.

At key stage 2, there are three papers. All pupils working at level 3 or above will be entered for papers A and B, unless there are exceptional circumstances. These papers assess levels 1 to 5. There are around 9 questions in each paper, and most are spread over a double page. The layout and presentation is child-friendly, with much use being made of line drawings and photographs showing children demonstrating or using equipment. An example question is shown in Figure 1. There is a third test, paper C, aimed at the small percentage of pupils working at level 6.

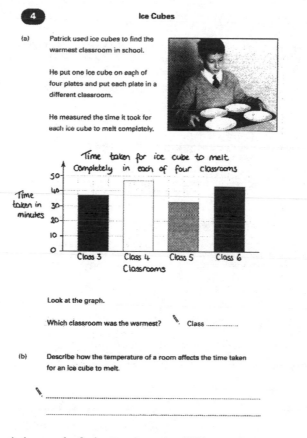

Figure 1: An example of a key stage 2 question (1999 paper A, tier 3-5)

8.   The drawing shows a boy with a bow and arrow. He is holding the **arrow** and
     pulling it back.

(a) Two horizontal forces act on the arrow. These are the force exerted by
     the boy's hand and the force exerted by the string. The arrow is **not**
     moving.

     The boy pulls the arrow with a force of 150 N. What is the size of the
     force exerted by the string on the arrow?

                                                                              1 mark

     _____ N

(b) When the boy lets go of the arrow, it starts to move forward.
     Explain why it starts to move.

                                                                              1 mark

     _____

     _____

(c) The arrow flies across a field and hits a target.

     Two forces act on the arrow while it is in the air. Air resistance acts in
     the opposite direction to the movement, and gravity acts downwards.
     These two forces **cannot** balance each other, even when they are the
     same size. Why is this?

                                                                              1 mark

     _____

     _____

(d) The arrow has a sharp pointed end. When the arrow hits the target,
     the sharp point exerts a very large pressure on the target.
     Why does a sharp pointed end exert a larger pressure than a blunt end?

                                                                              1 mark

     _____

     _____

Figure 2: An example of a key stage 3 question (2000 paper 1, tier 5-7)

The future of science in the curriculum

Over the last few decades, science education has undergone many changes. At the start of this section it was noted that the foremost role for science in the curriculum is not primarily to train future scientists but to provide an education in scientific literacy for the whole population. However, this concern for 'science for all' is relatively recent. The content of the current science curriculum is rooted in a 'science for specialists'. Historically, it was heavily influenced by the needs of universities and of the examination boards, and aimed at the more academic pupils, particularly boys. This change over the last few decades from a 'science for specialists' to a 'science for all' has had many successes but also difficulties. It is these difficulties that lie at the heart of many of the concerns about the current curriculum and that are likely to drive the next changes in the curriculum.

One of the key findings from research is that although pupils may perform well on tests and examinations, there are fundamental difficulties in their understanding of many science concepts. Many people have drawn the conclusion from this that the curriculum is far too overloaded with content, which inevitably leads to a superficial understanding. Research findings in many different countries show remarkable consistency, and the implications for the content of the curriculum are of concern to science educators worldwide. How can we choose the key aspects of scientific knowledge so the big ideas can be understood without becoming lost in the detail? How can motivation to study science be sustained? It seems that the curiosity and enthusiasm that primary school pupils demonstrate in science is not maintained into the later years of secondary school.

Practical work has a prominent place in science in schools; since experimentation is an important aspect in the construction of scientific knowledge. However, its role in the learning of science needs its own justification – it cannot simply be taken for granted. One justification put forward is that through undertaking investigations pupils can experience what it is like to be a scientist and will understand better how science is done. They are learning about science, not just learning science, and this is a central part of being scientifically literate.

Although practical work now has a prominent place in science in schools, research has shown that laboratory work on its own cannot always provide the contexts in which pupils can understand the nature of science. Previous versions of the National Curriculum have been criticised for being too narrow and prescriptive; the specification may have made it easier to assess pupils' investigations, but at the expense of presenting a distorted view of the way that science is actually done. The national curriculum 2000–2005 has attempted to broaden the vision of what scientific enquiry entails. How successful this has been will be the focus of a number of evaluation studies during this period.

There have been a number of different initiatives aimed at developing an understanding of what science is. These include studying historical and contemporary examples of scientific research, the relationship between science and technology, ethical issues in science, the role and importance of science on everyday life, or in risk assessment and decision-making. The current National Curriculum includes these kinds of areas, but they are not given great prominence in the classroom. Assessment of the National Curriculum also focuses strongly on scientific content, and increasingly it is assessment that determines what is done in the classroom. There are, however, many who advocate that these broader aspects of science that will take on an increasing significance as the need for a scientifically literate society becomes even more pressing.

The non-core foundation subjects

This chapter gives an outline of the National Curriculum in each of the non-core foundation subjects beyond the core subjects of English, mathematics and science. These have to be taught at key stage 3 but not all are compulsory in the GCSE examination preparation years of key stage 4 (see Chapter 1).

Design and technology

Design and technology has been in the National Curriculum for ten years and has now become established as an important non-core foundation subject. This has not been an easy process, however. Design and technology was a new subject in 1990 and there was much discussion and debate about its purpose and its content. Early debates centred on the balance between the theoretical and practical aspects of the subject, and on its vocational or general educational purposes. There were also concerns that teachers from the various contributing subjects did not have the experience to teach all aspects of the subject, especially in primary schools. Under the umbrella of 'technology', the first National Curriculum brought together the previously separate subjects of art; business studies; craft, design and technology; home economics (including textiles) and information technology. In later revisions, and in practice, 'design and technology' became a joint venture between craft, design and technology and home economics (including textiles). Many people are unfamiliar with this new approach to the subject and it is described here, therefore, in more detail than some other subjects.

These initial concerns have now largely been resolved and design and technology is a popular subject with pupils. The 2000 National

Curriculum for England contains the following statement to describe the importance of design and technology to the curriculum:

> ...[it] prepares pupils to participate in tomorrow's rapidly changing technologies. They learn to think and intervene creatively to improve quality of life. The subject calls for pupils to become autonomous and creative problem solvers, as individuals and members of a team. They must look for needs, wants and opportunities and respond to them by developing a range of ideas and making products and systems. They combine practical skills with an understanding of aesthetics, social and environmental issues, function and industrial practices. As they do so, they reflect on and evaluate present and past design and technology, its uses and effects. Through design and technology, all pupils can become discriminating and informed users of products and become innovators.

The study of design and technology includes working with resistant (i.e. hard) materials such as wood and metal; compliant materials such as plastics and textiles; electronics, and food. Graphic skills should be taught through all these areas, and this area is offered separately as an examination subject (graphics products). Most schools offer opportunities for pupils to work with all these materials, but some omit experiences in food and/or textiles. In National Curriculum 2000 the Government states that it:

> ... believes that schools should be encouraged to look for opportunities to teach both food and textiles as part of the range of contrasting materials that pupils should use ...

Design and technology is a subject which brings together intellectual skills, knowing something, and practical skills, doing something. It emphasises the importance of the ability to *apply* knowledge and skills, and provides opportunities for pupils to develop their abilities to innovate, to make decisions and to create new solutions. Through the 'design' strand of the work it encourages pupils to evaluate objects, and become critical users and consumers. The subject plays a unique role in helping pupils to develop personal qualities and competences through these ways of working.

Design and technology can also contribute to helping pupils develop an awareness of business and industrial practices, and the ways in which technological developments can change the workplace and influence lifestyles, through the requirement to use computer-aided design and manufacture as an integral part of their learning. Pupils will also be developing an awareness of the influences of society on technological developments, with the need to consider aesthetics, social and environmental issues in their designing and making, and in looking at technology from different historical and cultural perspectives.

The programme of study is the section of the National Curriculum that sets out what pupils should be taught. In design and technology it requires that pupils acquire knowledge and understanding of materials and components, systems and control, and structures, which they can apply when developing ideas, planning and making products and when evaluating products. They are also expected to draw on knowledge and understanding from other areas of the curriculum, where relevant.

The knowledge and understanding required at key stage 1 includes that pupils be taught:

(a)   about the working characteristics of materials (*for example, folding paper to make it stiffer*)

(b)   how mechanisms can be used in different ways (*for example, wheels and axles*).

At key stage 3 this becomes more complex, for example, in relation to materials and components, pupils should be taught:

(a)   to consider physical and chemical properties and working characteristics of a range of common and modern materials

(b)   that materials and components can be classified according to their properties and working characteristics

(c)   that materials and components can be combined, processed and finished to create more useful properties and particular aesthetic effects

(d)   how multiple copies can be made of the same product.

Throughout the key stages there is a requirement that pupils be taught the knowledge, skills and understanding outlined in the programme of study through:

(a)   product analysis (this refers to evaluation of existing products)

(b)   focused practical tasks that develop a range of techniques, skills, processes and knowledge

(c)   design and make assignments, which in key stage 1 should use a range of materials, including food, items that can be put together, products and textiles. In key stage 3, assignments should be set in different contexts and in key stage 4 should include activities related to industrial practices.

There is also a general requirement that pupils be taught about health and safety issues and risk assessment when working with tools, equipment, and materials in practical environments.

The attainment targets in the National Curriculum describe what pupils should achieve as a result of following the programmes of study. The attainment target for design and technology has eight levels which covers pupils from key stage 1 to key stage 3, and one additional level of 'exceptional performance'. At key stage 4, attainment is covered by examination requirements.

The new attainment target includes aspects of both designing and making. For example, to achieve **level 2** in their work:

> Pupils generate ideas and plan what to do next, based on their experience of working with materials and components. They use models, pictures and words to describe their designs. They select appropriate tools, techniques and materials, explaining their choices. They use tools and assemble, join and combine materials and components in a variety of ways. They recognise what they have done well as their work progresses and suggest things they could do better in the future.

At the higher level, **level 5**, they should:

> ... draw on and use various sources of information. They
> clarify their ideas through discussion, drawing and modelling.
> They use their understanding of the characteristics of familiar
> products when developing and communicating their own
> ideas. They work from their own detailed plans, modifying
> them where appropriate. They work with a range of tools,
> materials, equipment, components and processes with some
> precision. They check their work as it develops and modify
> their approach in the light of progress. They test and evaluate
> their products, showing that they understand the situations in
> which their designs will have to function and are aware of
> resources as a constraint. They evaluate their products and their
> use of information sources.

Exemptions from design and technology

Design and technology is a non-core foundation subject in the
National Curriculum, and as such should be studied by all pupils
aged 5-16. However, there are now regulations in place which allow
schools to 'disapply' the National Curriculum requirements for
certain pupils. Individual pupils may be exempted from studying
design and technology if a school wishes to:

- provide wider opportunities for work-related learning than are
  possible alongside the full statutory requirement
- allow pupils making significantly less progress than their peers
  to study fewer National Curriculum subjects in order to
  consolidate their learning across the curriculum
- respond to pupils' individual strengths and talents by allowing
  them to emphasise a particular curriculum area by exchanging
  a statutory subject for a further course in that curriculum area

These regulations are intended to apply to only a few individual
pupils and should not cause large numbers to omit this subject from
their studies. Schools will provide more detailed guidance on this.

Design and technology: Wales

In Wales, study of design and technology is compulsory at key stages 1, 2 and 3, but is optional at key stage 4.

In the programme of study, each key stage begins with a focus statement. These summarise the learning and teaching for each key stage and state that pupils' design and technology capability should be developed through:

> ...*combining designing and making skills with knowledge and understanding in order to design and make products.*

At key stages 1 and 2, what pupils should be taught is described under the headings of knowledge and understanding; designing skills; and making skills. At key stage 3 the headings are systems and control; structures; materials; designing skills; and making skills. At key stage 3 they are required to include the use of CAD/CAM in their designing and making.

The programme of study states that pupils should be taught through investigation and evaluation of familiar products, focused practical tasks and design and make activities. They are required to work with a range of materials, including wood, metal, plastics, textiles and food, and with control systems and structures.

There are a number of common requirements in the Welsh National Curriculum:

- Curriculum Cymreig, knowledge and understanding of the cultural, economic, environmental, historical and linguistic characteristics of Wales
- Communication skills
- Mathematical skills
- Information technology skills
- Problem–solving skills
- Creative skills
- Personal and social education

Where there are opportunities within the design and technology curriculum for one of these areas to be addressed, this is indicated in the programme of study with a symbol.

There is one attainment target, design and technology, which has eight levels. Examples of levels 2 and 5 are set out below.

Level 2

Pupils generate ideas and plan what to do next, based on their experience of working with materials and components. They use models, pictures and words to describe their designs. They select appropriate tools, techniques and materials, explaining their choices. They use tools and assemble, join and combine materials and components in a variety of ways. They recognise what they have done well as their work progresses, and suggest things they could do better in the future.

Level 5

Pupils generate ideas and recognise that their designs have to meet a range of different needs. They make realistic plans for achieving their aims. They clarify ideas when asked and use words, labelled sketches and models to communicate the details of their designs. They think ahead about the order of their work, choosing appropriate tools, equipment, materials, components and techniques. They use tools and equipment with some accuracy to cut and shape materials and to put together components. They identify where evaluation of the design and make process and their products has led to improvements.

Technology and design: Northern Ireland

The curriculum for technology and design in Northern Ireland is significantly different from that of England, although a number of similarities exist. In the introduction to the programme of study, designing is identified as a key activity and is said to require pupils:

> *To bring together and apply knowledge, understanding and skills relating to materials and components, energy and control, and manufacturing. Within the design activities there should be opportunities to analyse, investigate and generate ideas, and to evaluate those ideas.*

Areas covered by the programme of study are:

- communicating, including oral, written and graphic communication
- planning, where pupils plan their own work in a logical and organised manner
- appraising, where pupils review and refine their design work and skills in relation to manufacturing
- materials and components
- energy and control, which is considered to be central to technology and design activities, this includes electronic and mechanical control systems
- electronic systems and control
- mechanical systems and control
- computer control.

The main difference between the Northern Irish and English curricula is that technology and design requires pupils to work only with wood, metals and plastics (textiles may be used as an additional material) and there is a stronger emphasis on control systems. Food work is carried out in home economics, which is a separate subject in the Northern Ireland specification for the National Curriculum.

Technology and design is also required to contribute to a number of cross-curricular themes: education for mutual understanding/cultural heritage; health education; information technology; economic awareness and careers education. The National Curriculum illustrates how these may be covered.

There is one attainment target, technology and design capability, which has eight levels. The attainment target states that pupils should develop, in parallel, their ability to:

■   Apply knowledge and understanding;

■   Communicate effectively;

■   Manipulate a range of materials and components to make products;

■   Use energy to drive and control products they design

Despite the differences in some areas of content, the underlying rationale for design and technology, and the emphasis on process, is the same across the three countries. Pupils' experiences will differ mainly in the materials that they work with, but the abilities and capabilities that they develop will broadly be the same.

Information and communication technology

In the period 2000 to 2005 teachers and schools will be experiencing significant changes in the way information and communication technologies are used. Between 2000 and 2003 all teachers in the UK will have had the opportunity to take part in specialist training to equip them with the skills to use the new technologies in all aspects of their teaching. Over the same period, an extensive programme of equipping schools with the necessary hardware and software is also taking place. This is one of the most interesting and potentially valuable areas of school development. It is also one of the most challenging. Many teachers and parents come from the generations that grew up without computers. They are understandably cautious about the way pupils can exploit the new forms of communication. Yet most young people see all forms of technological communication as 'cool'. Whatever the ups and downs in the new e-economy and whatever the possibilities presented by as yet unimagined technologies, we appear to be moving into a new age of communications. It is affecting all aspects of social and economic life, with a particular impact on the structure of employment.

The National Curriculum has a requirement that all pupils at each of the key stages study information and communication technology. Young people need to be skilled in the way technologies are used and the value of information and communication technologies in studying a range of subjects. In terms of its importance, the National Curriculum says the following:

> *Information and communication technology (ICT) prepares pupils to participate in a rapidly changing world in which work and other activities are increasingly transformed by access to varied and developing technology. Pupils use ICT tools to find, explore, analyse, exchange and present information responsibly, creatively and with discrimination. They learn how to employ ICT to enable rapid access to ideas and experiences from a wide range of people, communities and cultures. Increased capability in the use of ICT promotes initiative and independent learning, with pupils being able to make informed judgements about when and where to use ICT to best effect, and to consider its implications for home and work both now and in the future.*

The programmes of study are set out under four headings:

- Finding things out
- Developing ideas and making them happen
- Exchanging and sharing information
- Reviewing, modifying and evaluating work as it progresses.

As in all subjects, there is a progress development of each of these areas across the key stages. Given the new nature of the subject and the unfamiliarity of many people with the processes and content involved, the full text for each of the key stages is set out below:

Key stage 1

Finding things out

1   Pupils should be taught how to:

(a)   gather information from a variety of sources (for example, people, books, databases, CD-ROMs, videos and TV)

(b) enter and store information in a variety of forms (for example, storing information in a prepared database, saving work)

(c) retrieve information that has been stored (for example using a CD-ROM, loading saved work).

Developing ideas and making things happen

2   Pupils should be taught:

(a) to use text, tables, images and sound to develop their ideas

(b) how to select from and add to information they have retrieved for particular purposes

(c) how to plan and give instructions to make things happen (for example, placing instructions in the right order)

(d) to try things out and explore what happens in real and imaginary situations (for example, trying out different colours on an image, using an adventure game or simulation).

Exchanging and sharing information

3   Pupils should be taught:

(a) how to share their ideas by presenting information in a variety of forms (for example, text, images, tables, sounds)

(b) to present their completed work effectively (for example, for public display).

Reviewing, modifying and evaluating work as it progresses

4   Pupils should be taught to:

(a) review what they have done to help them develop their ideas

(b) describe the effects of their actions

(c) talk about what they might change in future work.

Key stage 2

Finding things out

1   Pupils should be taught:

   (a) to talk about what information they need and how they
       can find and use it (for example, searching the internet or
       a CD-ROM, using printed material, asking people)

   (b) how to prepare information for development using ICT,
       including selecting suitable sources, finding information,
       classifying it and checking it for accuracy (for example,
       finding information from books or newspapers, creating a
       class database, classifying by characteristics and purposes,
       checking the spelling of names is consistent)

   (c) to interpret information, to check it is relevant and
       reasonable and to think about what might happen if there
       were any errors or omissions.

Developing ideas and making things happen

2   Pupils should be taught:

   (a) how to develop and refine ideas by bringing together,
       organising and reorganising text, tables, images and sound
       as appropriate (for example, desktop publishing,
       multimedia presentations)

   (b) how to create, test, improve and refine sequences of
       instructions to make things happen and to monitor events
       and respond to them (for example, monitoring
       changes in temperature, detecting light levels and turning
       on a light)

   (c) to use simulations and explore models in order to answer
       'What if...?' questions, to investigate and evaluate the
       effect of changing values and to identify patterns and
       relationships (for example, simulation software,
       spreadsheet models).

Exchanging and sharing information

3   Pupils should be taught:

(a) how to share and exchange information in a variety of forms, including e-mail (for example, displays, posters, animations, musical compositions)

(b) to be sensitive to the needs of the audience and think carefully about the content and quality when communicating information (for example, work for a presentation to other pupils, writing for parents, publishing on the internet).

Reviewing, modifying and evaluating work as it progresses

4   Pupils should be taught to:

(a) review what they and others have done to help them develop their ideas

(b) describe and talk about the effectiveness of their work with ICT, comparing it with other methods and considering the effect it has on others (for example, the impact made by a desktop-published newsletter or poster)

(c) talk about how they could improve future work.

Key stage 3

Finding things out

1   Pupils should be taught:

(a) to be systematic in considering the information they need and to discuss how it will be used

(b) how to obtain information well matched to purpose by selecting appropriate sources, using and refining search methods and questioning the plausibility and value of the information found

(c) how to collect, enter, analyse and evaluate quantitative and qualitative information, checking its accuracy (for example, carrying out a survey of local traffic, analysing data gathered in fieldwork).

Developing ideas and making things happen

2   Pupils should be taught:

(a)   to develop and explore information, solve problems and derive new information for particular purposes (for example, deriving totals from raw data, reaching conclusions by exploring information)

(b)   how to use ICT to measure, record, respond to and control events by planning, testing and modifying sequences of instructions (for example, using automatic weather stations, datalogging in fieldwork and experiments, using feedback to control devices)

(c)   how to use ICT to test predictions and discover patterns and relationships, by exploring, evaluating and developing models and changing their rules and values

(d)   to recognise where groups of instructions need repeating and to automate frequently used processes by constructing efficient procedures that are fit for purpose (for example, templates and macros, control procedures, formulae and calculations in spreadsheets).

Exchanging and sharing information

3   Pupils should be taught:

(a)   how to interpret information and to reorganise and present it in a variety of forms that are fit for purpose (for example, information about a charitable cause presented in a leaflet for a school fundraising event)

(b)   to use a range of ICT tools efficiently to draft, bring together and refine information and create good-quality presentations in a form that is sensitive to the needs of particular audiences and suits the information content

(c)   how to use ICT, including e-mail, to share and exchange information effectively (for example, web publishing, video conferencing).

Reviewing, modifying and evaluating work as it progresses

4   Pupils should be taught to:

(a)   reflect critically on their own and others' uses of ICT to help them develop and improve their ideas and the quality of their work

(b)   share their views and experiences of ICT, considering the range of its uses and talking about its significance to individuals, communities and society

(c)   discuss how they might use ICT in future work and how they would judge its effectiveness, using relevant technical terms

(d)   be independent and discriminating when using ICT.

Key stage 4

Finding things out

1   Pupils should be taught:

(a)   how to analyse the requirements of tasks, taking into account the information they need and the ways they will use it

(b)   to be discriminating in their use of information sources and ICT tools.

Developing ideas and making things happen

2   Pupils should be taught to:

(a)   use ICT to enhance their learning and the quality of their work

(b)   use ICT effectively to explore, develop and interpret information and solve problems in a variety of subjects and contexts

(c) apply, as appropriate, the concepts and techniques of using ICT to measure, record, respond to, control and automate events

(d) apply, as appropriate, the concepts and techniques of ICT-based modelling, considering their advantages and limitations against other methods.

Exchanging and sharing information

3   Pupils should be taught to:

(a) use information sources and ICT tools effectively to share, exchange and present information in a variety of subjects and contexts

(b) consider how the information found and developed using ICT should be interpreted and presented in forms that are sensitive to the needs of particular audiences, fit for purpose and suit the information content.

Reviewing, modifying and evaluating work as it progresses

4   Pupils should be taught to:

(a) evaluate the effectiveness of their own and others' uses of information sources and ICT tools, using the results to improve the quality of their work and to inform future judgements

(b) reflect critically on the impact of ICT on their own and others' lives, considering the social, economic, political, legal, ethical and moral issues (for example, changes to working practices, the economic impact of e-commerce, the implications of personal information gathered, held and exchanged using ICT)

(c) use their initiative to find out about and exploit the potential of more advanced or new ICT tools and information sources (for example, new sites on the internet, new or upgraded application software).

It is very important to remember that information and communications technology is not necessarily taught as a separate subject. Pupils will be expected normally to cover the knowledge, skills and understanding linked above, through the range of other subjects that they study in the National Curriculum. In science or geography, for example, a data handling package may be used to record, analyse and evaluate data for fieldwork. Spreadsheet applications have many uses in mathematics. Learning in all subjects will be helped by well-planned use of world-wide web resources, some particularly so. Every aspect of the teaching of history now has multiple well-developed web resources to enrich a pupil's understanding.

Young children are now expected to become familiar with the keyboard and the way computers can help their learning. In reception classes, for example, a class may work on using a word bank through discussing the words they see around them (labels, signs, and posters). Pupils could be shown how to select words from a word bank, using a mouse, and then make the computer say a word. At the end of the activity pupils might be expected to use a word bank to create simple sentences.

There are six levels for the attainment target for information and communication technology. Examples of levels 2 and 5 indicate the progression expected for primary to secondary schooling.

Level 2

Pupils use ICT to organise and classify information and to present their findings. They enter, save and retrieve work. They use ICT to help them generate, amend and record their work and share their ideas in different forms, including text, tables, images and sound. They plan and give instructions to make things happen and describe the effects. They use ICT to explore what happens in real and imaginary situations. They talk about their experiences of ICT both inside and outside school.

Level 5

Pupils select the information they need for different purposes, check its accuracy and organise it in a form suitable for processing. They use ICT to structure, refine and present information in different forms and styles for specific purposes and audiences. They exchange information and ideas with others in a variety of ways, including using e-mail. They create sequences of instructions to control events, and understand the need to be precise when framing and sequencing instructions. They understand how ICT devices with sensors can be used to monitor and measure external events. They explore the effects of changing the variables in an ICT-based model. They discuss their knowledge and experience of using ICT and their observations of its use outside school. They assess the use of ICT in their work and are able to reflect critically in order to make improvements in subsequent work.

Given that this subject area is covered in all the other subjects, schools are bound to have different strategies and approaches to teaching and to assessing the subject. They receive a great deal of advice about developing a policy for what is now normally called 'ICT'. It is important to look at school-specific documentation on the curriculum to see the particular way in which this subject is taught.

History

History is now firmly established in the National Curriculum. This was welcomed by history teachers as a move which recognised the value of history's contribution to a 'broad and balanced education' and preparation for adult life.

The importance of history is set out in the National Curriculum as follows:

> *History fires pupils' curiosity about the past in Britain and the wider world. Pupils consider how the past influences the present, what past societies were like, how these societies organised their politics, and what beliefs and cultures influenced people's actions. As they do this, pupils*

*develop a chronological framework for their knowledge of significant
events and people. They see the diversity of human experience, and
understand more about themselves as individuals and members of
society. What they learn can influence their decisions about personal
choices, attitudes and values. In history, pupils find evidence, weigh it
up and reach their own conclusions. To do this they need to be able to
research, sift through evidence, and argue for their point of view –
skills that are prized in adult life.*

Any subject which suggests that study will allow the individuals to
know more about themselves or their role in society and refers to
attitudes and values is bound to court controversy. There is an
ongoing debate, for example, about the place of British history. How
much time should it occupy in comparison to European or world
events? What is the balance between knowing the facts or story
(Magna Carta, Henry V, Nelson, the origins of the Parliamentary
forms of democracy) as opposed to understanding the methods of
history? How you investigate the past. What evidence is reliable for
making judgements? At a time when traditional values and traditional
identities (family, class, ethnicity) are fragmented and questioned, it is
hardly surprising that school history, together with the values it
enshrines, is an area of controversy. What is of more significance is
that as areas within the United Kingdom struggle with their identity,
England, Wales and Northern Ireland each have slight differences of
emphases within their History National Curricula.

National Curriculum history draws, like many subjects, on the
academic tradition of history which is found widely in British
universities. This places a premium on research and in archives and
other sources, the authenticity of documents and the reliability of
witnesses, and the need for substantiating evidence and countervailing
evidence. Underpinning the content of history are the methods of
analysing, interpreting and recording history. This historical
methodology requires the rigorous critical analysis of historical
evidence, together with an understanding of the central concepts of
history: what caused events, how events change over time, and the
motivations of the different individuals and groups participating in
historical events. School history is required to cover local, national

and world history. It allows history to build from pupils' own experience. It shows that localities and regions have national settings and that national history exists in an increasingly global context.

The knowledge, skills and understanding for history

In England, Northern Ireland and Wales, the knowledge, skills and understanding for history cover the same range of historical concepts and skills (time, change, continuity, similarity and difference, source evaluation and different interpretations of the past), although some have different titles and focuses:

England	Northern Ireland	Wales
Chronological understanding	Chronological awareness	Chronological awareness
Knowledge and understanding of events, people and changes in the past	Range and depth of historical knowledge and understanding	Historical knowledge and understanding
Historical interpretation	Interpretations of history (not at key stage 1)	Interpretations of history
Historical enquiry	Historical enquiry (not at key stage 1)	Historical enquiry
Organisation and communication	Organisation and communication	Organisation and communication

The focus and breadth of study at key stages 1, 2 and 3 in England, Northern Ireland and Wales

At each key stage (1–3), pupils are required to be taught the knowledge, skills and understanding of history through a given focus, study unit or breadth of study. The content of these is not specified in detail, and it is important to remember that the names, terms and organising concepts of history are open to wide interpretation. So, for example, although the history National Curriculum for England sets out that key stage 3 should include a study of 'Britain 1066–1500 – a study of major features of Britain's medieval past: the development of the monarchy, and significant events and characteristic features of the lives of the people throughout the British Isles, including the local area if appropriate', the exact events that teachers choose to focus on can vary widely. In considering the development of the monarchy they may choose to explore gender and legitimacy, 'better a woman than a bastard', through a consideration of Queen Matilda, or consider the role of queens in medieval England's international diplomacy. Examples from the programme of study are set out below.

Key Stage 1

England: history. key stage1. Breadth of study	Northern Ireland: history key stage1	Wales: history key stage 1. Focus of study
Pupils should be taught: ■ changes in their own lives and the way of life of their family or others around them; ■ the way of life of people in the more distant past who lived in the local area or elsewhere in Britain; ■ the lives of significant men,	An introduction to history. Aspects of the following three themes should be taught throughout the key stage: ■ personal history; ■ personalities, events and celebrations; ■ topics.	Pupils should be taught about: ■ changes in their lives and those of adults and localities familiar to them; ■ people and events from both the history of their own area and that of Wales, Britain and other countries.

women and children drawn from the history of Britain and the wider world; ■ past events from the history of Britain and the wider world.		

Key stage 2

England: history. Key stage 2. Breadth of study	Northern Ireland: history key stage 2. Study units	Wales: history key stage 2. Focus of study
■ Local history study – an investigation of how an aspect of the local area has changed over a long period of time, or how the locality was affected by a significant national or local event or development, or by the work of a significant individual. ■ British history – pupils should be taught about the	■ Life in early times: Middle Stone Age, New Stone Age, and one of the following topics – a local dimension, a topic linked to 'Life in early times', a topic of their own choice unrelated to 'Life in Early Times', a local study of their choice unrelated to 'Life in early times'. ■ The Vikings – the unit should	■ Life in early Wales and Britain. ■ Life in Britain in either Tudor or Stuart times. ■ Life in modern Wales and Britain. ■ In-depth study – a historical topic in a local context. ■ Pupils should be taught about change and continuity in at least one aspect of life, either houses or

Romans, Anglo-Saxons and Vikings, Britain and the wider world in Tudor times and either Victorian Britain or Britain since 1930. This study should cover aspects of the histories of England, Ireland, Scotland and Wales; and put the history of Britain in its European and world context. ■ A European history study – ancient Greece. ■ A world history study – a study of the key features including the everyday lives of men, women and children of a past society selected from ancient Egypt, Ancient Sumer, the Assyrian Empire, the Indus Valley, the Maya, Benin, or the Aztecs.	focus on the nature of Viking society in Scandinavia and the impact of Viking raiders and settlers in Ireland and elsewhere. ■ Life in Victorian times – the unit should focus on the lives of people in both town and country at different levels of Victorian society in both Britain and Ireland, and some of the significant changes and developments of the Victorian era.	households, or food and farming, or writing and reading, or transport by land or sea over all the periods studies.

Key stage 3

England: history key stage 3. Breadth of study	Northern Ireland: history key stage 3. Study units	Wales: history key stage 3. Focus of study
■ Britain 1066–1500. ■ Britain 1500–1750. ■ Britain 1750–1900. ■ A European study before 1914. ■ A world study before 1900. ■ A world study after 1900. In their study of local, British, European and world history, pupils should be taught about: **(a)** significant events, people and changes from the recent and more distant past **(b)** history from a variety of perspectives, including political, religious, social,	■ The Normans and the medieval world: the Norman conquest, aspects of medieval society, the Normans in Ireland. ■ Rivalry and conflict – the causes of European rivalries and conflict in the late 16th century; Crown and Parliament, Ireland c. 1600–1700. ■ Union to partition – social and economic change in Ireland and Britain, home rule and partition. ■ The twentieth-century world – the impact of world war; a	■ Wales and Britain in the medieval world c. 1000–1500. ■ Wales and Britain in the early modern world c. 1500–1760. ■ Wales in industrial Britain c. 1760–1914. ■ The twentieth-century world. ■ An aspect of local history. ■ One historical theme in depth: explorations and encounters, war and society, the world of work, revolutions, frontiers, migration and emigration, empires, sport and society.

cultural, aesthetic, economic, technological and scientific **(c)** aspects of the histories of England, Ireland, Scotland and Wales where appropriate **(d)** the history of Britain in its European and wider world context **(e)** some aspects of overview and others in-depth.	significant social development; a major event or person; a significant organisation. ■ Study units of the school's own choice: a place, event, personality or group of significance to the local area, or a local development, an historical theme over time, a significant turning point in history, a past European or non-European society.	

Assessment

There is one attainment target in history and this is described at eight levels. Levels 2 and 5 provide two examples:

Level 2

Pupils show their developing sense of chronology by using terms concerned with the passing of time, by placing events and objects in order, and by recognising that their own lives are different from the lives of people in the past. They show knowledge and understanding of aspects of the past beyond living memory, and of some of the main events and people they have studied. They are beginning to recognise that there are reasons why people in the past acted as they did. They are beginning to identify some of the different ways in which the past is represented. They observe or handle sources of information to answer questions about the past on the basis of simple observations.

Level 5

Pupils show increasing depth of factual knowledge and understanding of aspects of the history of Britain and the wider world. They use this to describe features of past societies and periods and to begin to make links between them. They describe events, people and changes. They describe and make links between events and changes and give reasons for, and results of, these events and changes. They know that some events, people and changes have been interpreted in different ways and suggest possible reasons for this. Using their knowledge and understanding, pupils are beginning to evaluate sources of information and identify those that are useful for particular tasks. They select and organise information to produce structured work, making appropriate use of dates and terms.

Pupils are, therefore, expected to make significant progress in the way they analyse and interpret historical events. A primary pupil in the early years is observing and handling information about the past whereas at junior secondary level they are selecting and organising information. At level 8, pupils are expected to use sources of information critically, carry out historical enquiries, and reach substantiated conclusions independently. It is important to remember that progress is represented by the pupils' understanding of the historical process and not the content. The old idea that Vikings are for primary classes and the first industrial revolution for the secondary school has long disappeared.

Geography

Geography, like other subjects in the National Curriculum, can stimulate lively national debate. Some critics have pointed to children's inadequate knowledge of countries and cities as evidence of declining educational standards. Others, however, have pointed to the futility of what has been termed a 'capes and bays' approach to the subject. The ability to reel off a list of capital cities or major rivers, it is argued, is as empty an exercise as knowing the dates of the Kings and Queens of England. Inevitably the National Curriculum in geography attracted some controversy, although in a more muted form than in subjects such as English or History.

The context of, and approach to, teaching geography have undergone significant changes in the last few decades. Many parents will remember drawing detailed regional maps, with symbols to show where coal mines or shoe manufacturing existed. They might also remember diagrams of U-shaped valleys gouged out by the ice of a glacial period. An interest in regions and the physical characteristics of the earth still exists, but in the context of some new perspectives that have profoundly influenced the way the subject is approached. There have been, for example, important developments to strengthen the scientific basis of the subject. Secondly, in a contrasting but complementary way, there has been a move to focus on issues and problems that go beyond the particular characteristics of regions or countries. The decline in world stocks of national fuel resources, poverty across significant parts of the globe, and the economic interdependence between developed and underdeveloped countries would be three examples.

The importance of geography is defined in the National Curriculum as follows:

> *Geography provokes and answers questions about the natural and human worlds, using different scales of enquiry to view them from different perspectives. It develops knowledge of places and environments throughout the world, an understanding of maps, and a range of investigative and problem-solving skills both inside and outside the classroom. As such, it prepares pupils for adult life and employment.*

Geography is a focus within the curriculum for understanding and resolving issues about the environment and sustainable development. It is also an important link between the natural and social sciences. As pupils study geography, they encounter different societies and cultures. This helps them realise how nations rely on each other. It can inspire them to think about their own place in the world, their values, and their rights and responsibilities to other people and the environment.

The specification for geography is set out under four headings:

- geographical enquiry and skills
- knowledge and understanding of places
- knowledge and understanding of patterns and processes
- knowledge and understanding of environmental change and sustainable development.

These general themes are progressively developed across the key stages. At key stage 1, for example, pupils should learn how to recognise changes in the environment such as those caused by traffic pollution and they should learn how to recognise the ways in which the environment can be improved and sustained. They might look at a local scheme to restrict the number of vehicles in a particular area. At key stage 1, pupils should study the locality of the school and a contrasting area either in the UK or overseas.

In key stage 3, pupils consider more complex forms of environmental change, for example deforestation and soil erosion and they also learn different approaches to managing such problems. They have to look at two countries in significantly different states of economic development and understand the regional differences that exist within these countries and the causes and consequences of such differences.

Access to the world-wide web provides geography teachers with a vast range of resources. Pupils, for example, in key stage 3 could use an automatic weather station for datalogging weather information for comparison with similar data from other places. Geography, more than most subjects, allows pupils to explore and understand issues of globalisation which is increasingly recognised as a political, economic and social phenomena of great significance. There are a huge range of sites providing first class resources that explore a range of topics, and examples are given in the further sources of information section.

There is one attainment target in Geography, and this is described at eight levels. Levels 2 and 5 provide two examples:

Level 2

Pupils show their knowledge, skills and understanding in studies at a local scale. They describe physical and human features of places, and recognise and make observations about those features that give places their character. They show an awareness of places beyond their own locality. They express views on the environment of a locality and recognise how people affect the environment. They carry out simple tasks and select information using resources that are given to them. They use this information and their own observations to help them ask and respond to questions about places and environments. They begin to use appropriate geographical vocabulary.

Level 5

Pupils show their knowledge, skills and understanding in studies of a range of places and environments at more than one scale and in different parts of the world. They describe and begin to explain geographical patterns and physical and human processes. They describe how these processes can lead to similarities and differences in the environments of different places and in the lives of people who live there. They recognise some of the links and relationships that make places dependent on each other. They suggest explanations for the ways in which human activities cause changes to the environment and the different views people hold about them. They recognise how people try to manage environments sustainably. They explain their own views and begin to suggest relevant geographical questions and issues. Drawing on their knowledge and understanding, they select and use appropriate skills and ways of presenting information from the key stage 2 or 3 programme of study to help them investigate places and environments. They select information and sources of evidence, suggest plausible conclusions to their investigations and present their findings both graphically and in writing.

It is important to notice the progression in the wording. At the primary stage, children are observing their environment and beginning to develop a geographical vocabulary. In secondary schools, pupils are making connections, seeing the links between human activities and environmental change. The schemes of work and the activities that now feature in the geography classroom are aimed to ensure that an increasingly demanding but structured and coherent geography curriculum is offered to all pupils.

Modern foreign languages

Teaching and learning a language that can be used in the modern world is a key aspect of the National Curriculum. All pupils in key stage 3 must study a modern foreign language unless they have a statement of special educational needs that specifically excludes them from this. The vast majority of pupils also continue to study modern foreign languages at key stage 4, if only for a short course.

The National Curriculum sets out a specification as to why language learning is important:

> Through the study of a foreign language, pupils understand and appreciate different countries, cultures, people and communities – and as they do so, begin to think of themselves as citizens of the world as well as of the United Kingdom. Pupils also learn about the basic structures of language. They explore the similarities and differences between the foreign language they are learning and English or another language, and learn how language can be manipulated and applied in different ways. Their listening, reading and memory skills improve, and their speaking and writing become more accurate. The development of these skills, together with pupils' knowledge and understanding of the structure of language, lay the foundations for future study of other languages.

Assessment of modern foreign languages is against four separate attainment targets (ATs):

AT1	listening and responding
AT2	speaking
AT3	reading and responding
AT4	writing

The programme of study for modern foreign languages is fortunate to have been subjected to rather fewer changes than many other National Curriculum subjects over the years.

Each level description gives an idea of the performance that a pupil should characteristically demonstrate when working at that level.

At the end of key stage 3, teachers use the descriptions to identify the level that, *in their professional judgement*, best describes the performance of each pupil, taking into consideration the pupil's strengths and weaknesses across a range of contexts. They confirm the decision by checking the level immediately above and the one immediately below to make sure that they have chosen the 'best fit' This is not worked out as a percentage or any other mathematical calculation, nor is it based upon either a single piece of work or an exam.

Language departments will have their own marking policy for assessing work on a day-to-day basis in the context of the needs and achievements of their pupils. In modern foreign languages, the great majority of pupils are expected to reach level 5 or 6 by the end of key stage 3. At the end of key stage 4, performance is usually assessed through the GCSE examination.

Schools are required to offer:

> 'one or more of the official working languages of the European Union'.

In alphabetical order these are: *Danish, Dutch, Finnish, French, German, Modern Greek, Italian, Portuguese, Spanish, and Swedish.*

In addition, they may offer any other modern foreign language. Non-EU languages count as a non-core foundation subject only when they are offered to pupils alongside the possibility of studying an official working language of the EU. So a pupil may not necessarily study any of these EU languages but at least one of them must be on offer in the school.

Traditionally, the language most frequently offered by schools, as a first foreign language has been French. This is still the case, although a more diverse pattern is emerging in some schools and it is not unusual to find schools which have 'diversified' and offer German, Spanish, Italian, Urdu or other languages.

There remain some difficulties with this diversification policy. Concerns about staffing for all languages are far from resolved, as the majority of teachers entering the profession are French specialists. When pupils move on to other schools where less common languages are taught, there are problems of transition. A school choosing to offer say Italian may have only one specialist in that language. If they leave, a replacement is not always easily available.

The National Curriculum introduced in 2000 emphasises the importance of pupils being able to communicate in the target language. As anyone who travels knows, it is important to be able to make yourself understood, even if the exact structure of the sentences used may be incorrect. Over the last twenty years, language teaching has increasingly adopted what has been termed the 'communicative' approach. It was a reaction against the more traditional teaching that may have allowed pupils to express accurate sentences in a written form but left them tongue-tied in Calais. There has been some concern, however, that the emphasis had shifted too far away from grammatical understanding. It is now suggested you need to be able to have strategies for communicating in the target language but that this is helped if you have a knowledge of the basic structure of the language.

Statement 1b of the National Curriculum specifically addresses this concern:

> *Pupils should be taught the grammar of the target language and how to apply it.*

The structure of employment in the twenty-first century is likely to have a greater European and international character. The ability to communicate in a second or third language, or even to learn a new one quickly, could become crucial to many jobs. Teachers are required to use the Target language as much as possible and pupils are expected to respond in the target language in most situations.

The programme of study for modern foreign languages has four main sections:

- Acquiring knowledge and understanding of the target language
- Developing language skills
- Developing language learning skills
- Developing cultural awareness

There are also margin notes that, on one side give a brief general outline of the expectations of key stages 3 and 4, and on the other side point out where links may be made with other subjects.

Developing language skills, for both key stages 3 and 4, has ten subsections that specify particular requirements. These are:

(a) how to listen carefully for gist and detail

(b) correct pronunciation and intonation

(c) how to ask and answer questions

(d) how to initiate and develop conversations

(e) how to vary the target language to suit context, audience and purpose

(f) how to adapt language they already know for different contexts

(g) strategies for dealing with the unpredictable (for example, unfamiliar language, unexpected responses)

(h) techniques for skimming and for scanning written texts for information, including those from ICT-based sources

(i) how to summarise and report the main points of spoken or written texts, using notes where appropriate

(j) how to redraft their writing to improve its accuracy and presentation, including the use of ICT.

Each of the attainment targets is described in eight level descriptions. Level 2 in speaking illustrates the sort of progress that pupils should make in the early years of the secondary school. Level 5 shows the sort of progress they would be making a couple of years later:

Level 2

Pupils give short, simple responses to what they see and hear. They name and describe people, places and objects. They use set phrases (for example, to ask for help and permission). Their pronunciation may still be approximate and the delivery hesitant, but their meaning is clear.

Level 5

Pupils take part in short conversations, seeking and conveying information and opinions in simple terms. They refer to recent experiences or future plans, as well as everyday activities and interests. Although there may be some mistakes, pupils make themselves understood with little or no difficulty.

Increasing emphasis is being placed on the importance of language learning. Although the National Curriculum has helped boost language learning up to age 16, the numbers of pupils choosing to study a language at advanced level has been dropping. Some experimentation has been taking place to introduce modern foreign language learning in primary schools. The argument is that a strong foundation prior to the more self-conscious adolescent years may provide a spur to later learning. It is too soon to pass judgement on the outcomes. Similar attempts twenty or more years ago met with limited success. Finding staff with the language skills is a challenge. As Britain's economic and social links with Europe grow stronger, the value of language competence becomes increasingly significant. Over the next few years there are likely to be a number of initiatives to promote and improve teaching and learning across the range of languages.

Art and design

Art and design covers a wide variety of activities. It includes a craft element and, therefore, involves the use of a range of processes and materials. In a contemporary art and design class it might be possible to see traditional painting or collage activities as well as computer-aided graphic design, perhaps using digital camera images. There are strong links with design and technology, and in many schools links will be made between design activities taking place in the workshops and art studios.

The importance of art & design in the National Curriculum is that:

> Art and design stimulates creativity and imagination. It provides visual, tactile and sensory experiences and a unique way of understanding and responding to the world. Pupils use colour, form, texture, pattern and different materials and processes to communicate what they see, feel and think. Through art and design activities, they learn to make informed value judgements and aesthetic and practical decisions, becoming actively involved in shaping environments. They explore ideas and meanings in the work of artists, craftspeople and designers. They learn about the diverse roles and functions of art, craft and design in contemporary life, and in different times and cultures. Understanding, appreciation and enjoyment of the visual arts have the power to enrich our personal and public lives.

Art and design teachers are asked to develop four areas of knowledge, skills and understanding:

- exploring and developing ideas
- investigating and making art, craft and design

- evaluating and developing work
- knowledge and understanding.

Knowledge and understanding in this context refers to teaching and learning about visual and tactile elements, including colour, pattern and texture, materials and processes used in making art, craft and design and the differences and similarities in the work of artists, craftspeople and designers in different times and cultures.

Earlier versions of the National Curriculum specified which artists pupils should learn about, but in the National Curriculum 2000–2005 this has been dropped. It was seen as too prescriptive, giving insufficient flexibility for art teachers to develop their own sources and resources.

To achieve the necessary knowledge, skills and understanding, art and design should be taught through a range of activities, working individually and in groups. Emphasis is placed on exploring the local environment, particularly museums and art galleries, and from key stage 2 onwards, the use of the computer as well as the more traditional forms of painting, collage and printmaking are included. Schools have plentiful opportunities to develop particular strengths and areas of expertise and to exploit aspects of the local environment. Information about these should be available to parents.

There is one attainment target for art and design and this has been set out in six levels. To show pupils' progress, look at the differences between the attainment expected of primary pupils at level 2 and secondary pupils at level 5:

Level 2

Pupils explore ideas. They investigate and use a variety of materials and processes to communicate their ideas and meanings, and design and make images and artefacts. They comment on differences in others' work, and suggest ways of improving their own.

Level 5

Pupils explore ideas and select visual and other information. They use this in developing their work, taking account of the purpose. They manipulate materials and processes to communicate ideas and meanings and make images and artefacts, matching visual and tactile qualities to their intentions. They analyse and comment on ideas, methods and approaches used in their own and others' work, relating these to its context. They adapt and refine their work to reflect their own view of its purpose and meaning.

Art and design is not easy to assess. People have very wide responses to different forms of experience and the controversies that occur in the art world generally are to be found in the school world. What is the worth of a work by Tracey Emin or Damien Hurst compared to more traditional artists? Art and design teachers do have the opportunity to look at work from a variety of schools, particularly in the examination years. This allows some moderation of views so that the assessment of any particular pupil's work will go beyond the views of any individual teacher.

Music

Music has always played an important part in the life of schools. However, until relatively recently, more attention tended to be paid to musical activities that took place outside of the classroom (choirs, recorder groups, etc.) than to the teaching of curriculum music lessons. Particularly in secondary schools, a music teacher would be judged by how successful s/he was in developing extra-curricular groups and organising school concerts.

Relatively little importance was attached to what went on in curriculum music lessons. There were oases of good practice where teachers created opportunities for children to compose and perform music. However, much curriculum music tended to focus on class 'community' singing and inducting children through music appreciation classes into a body of 'great musical works'. In primary schools, music provision was patchy, being dependent upon whether there was a teacher on the staff who had the confidence and skills to teach the subject. Consequently, many people's memories of music lessons are less than positive.

Today, teachers in most schools still support orchestras and choirs outside of the curriculum, as well as ensembles such as rock groups and wind bands. The promotion of performing events is rightly still seen as an important aspect of the music teacher's role. However, in addition, music teachers are also responsible for teaching the music National Curriculum to *all* pupils from the ages of 5–14. A curriculum that now focuses on developing children's understanding of music through engaging with a range of musical styles as performers, composers and critical, analytical listeners.

The statement of the importance of music in the National Curriculum is set out as follows:

> *Music is a powerful, unique form of communication that can change the way pupils feel, think and act. It brings together intellect and feeling and enables personal expression, reflection and emotional development. As an integral part of culture, past and present, it helps pupils understand themselves and relate to others, forging important links between the home, school and the wider world. The teaching of music develops pupils' ability to listen and appreciate a wide variety of music and to make judgements about musical quality. It encourages active involvement in different forms of amateur music making, both individual and communal, developing a sense of group identity and togetherness. It also increases self-discipline and creativity, aesthetic sensitivity and fulfilment.*

There is one attainment target in music through which 'Teaching should ensure *that listening and applying knowledge and understanding* are developed through interrelated skills of *performing, composing and appraising*'. This holistic approach to music learning acknowledges that most musical activity involves the interaction of a range of musical activities. For example, performing and composing will require critical listening whilst critical listening requires appraising of music.

Progression in the music curriculum is provided for by grouping the development of knowledge, skills and understanding under four main headings that appear in each key stage. These are:

■ Controlling sounds through singing and playing – performing skills

■ Creating and developing musical ideas – composing skills

■ Responding and reviewing – appraising skills

■ Listening, and applying knowledge and understanding.

Pupils' *performing skills* are developed through singing and playing a range of 'tuned and untuned instruments'. These instruments will most often include glockenspiels, recorders, a range of Latin American percussion, and electronic keyboards. Historically, an implicit hierarchy of instruments has developed with vocal work and untuned percussion predominating in primary schools and electronic keyboards being the main instruments used in secondary schools. A consequence of this has been a decline in the standard of singing, particularly in secondary schools. The music National Curriculum seeks to arrest this decline by making the study of vocal skills a distinct aspect of the programmes of study. Thus, children are expected to:

■ 'use their voices expressively by singing songs and speaking chants and rhymes' (key stage 1)

■ 'sing songs in unison and two parts with clear diction, control of pitch and a sense of phrase and musical expression' (key stage 2)

■ 'sing unison and part songs developing vocal techniques and musical expression' (key stage 3).

In *composing*, the emphasis on progression through the key stages is in terms of the complexity of musical structures which children create and their awareness of different compositional styles. They are expected to progress from 'creating musical patterns' in key stage 1, to 'produce, develop and extend musical ideas selecting and combining resources within musical structures and given genres, styles and traditions' in key stage 3.

Appraising is the aspect of the programmes of study that most enables the integration of composing, performing and listening activities. Pupils are taught in key stage 1 to 'explore and express their ideas and feelings about music using movement and dance and expressive and musical language'. In key stage 2, they '... apply critical analysis to their own and others work', and in key stage 3 'adapt their own musical ideas and refine and improve their own and others' work'.

Listening is now an active exercise rather than one in which children are taught to 'appreciate' works of music. There are four main aspects to this part of the programme of study:

(a)   the ability to internalise and recall sounds - the development of aural memory;

(b)   understanding how musical elements (e.g. pitch, duration, dynamics, etc.) are organised expressively in music structures;

(c)   the different ways of making sounds – for example using voices, instruments and technology;

(d)   the way in which music and its creation is affected by its social and cultural context.

The listening aspect is not meant to be taught separately from other aspects of the programmes of study but to be part of integrated activities. So, for example, pupils' understanding of how musical elements are organised might be taught in the context of developing their composing skills. Similarly, through understanding how music is affected by cultural context, children will learn that there is not one set of criteria by which all music can be evaluated but that its success is often dependent upon how well it serves the purpose for which it is intended.

The differences in the breadth of study required for each key stage is minimal. This reflects the focus of the music National Curriculum on developing skills and deeper understanding of music through revisiting core activities and experiences, rather than focusing upon particular works of music. Thus, in all key stages pupils are required to be taught:

- through the integration of performing composing and appraising activities;
- through the use of musical and non-musical stimuli;
- in groups of different sizes and as a class;
- through a range of live and recorded music from different times and cultures.

From key stage 2, pupils have to be given the opportunity to use ICT to:

- capture, change and combine sounds (key stage 2);
- create, manipulate and refine sounds (key stage 3).

The distinctions between key stages 2 and 3 lie in the sophistication with which pupils are expected to use ICT in music and the resources available. The requirements for key stage 2 could be met through the creative use of a simple microphone and tape recorder or CD-ROM. In key stage 3, however, the requirement to 'create, manipulate and refine' implies access to more sophisticated digital technology including, perhaps, electronic keyboards, synthesisers, and sequencing software.

This is reflected in the progression across the music attainment target. Examples of levels 2 and 5 are set out below.

Level 2

Pupils recognise and explore how sounds can be organised. They sing with a sense of the shape of the melody, and perform simple patterns and accompaniments keeping to a steady pulse. They choose carefully and order sounds within simple structures such as beginning, middle, end, and in response to given starting points. They represent sounds with symbols and recognise how the musical elements can be used to create different moods and effects. They improve their own work.

Level 5

Pupils identify and explore musical devices and how music reflects time and place. They perform significant parts from memory and from notations with awareness of their own contribution, such as leading others, taking a solo part and/or providing rhythmic support. They improvise melodic and rhythmic material within given structures, use a variety of notations and compose music for different occasions using appropriate musical devices, such as melody, rhythms, chords and structures. They analyse and compare musical features. They evaluate how venue, occasion and purpose affects the way music is created, performed and heard. They refine and improve their work.

Whatever resources are available, however, the overriding message of the music National Curriculum is that children should be experiencing music first hand through composing and performing it.

Physical education

Physical education traditionally attracts very contrasting responses from children. For some, stimulated and enthused by individual or team sports, it can be the high point of the curriculum. For others, it can be just the reverse, particularly where a cross-country run and compulsory shower is part of the experience! The more punitive approach, however, is becoming a very rare experience and physical education teachers now embrace a very different approach to the subject. The National Curriculum is much more than forward and backward rolls, jumping the horse, or scaling a rope. Look, for example, at the rationale for the importance of physical education.

> *Physical education develops pupils' physical competence and confidence, and their ability to use these to perform in a range of activities. It promotes physical skilfulness, physical development and a knowledge of the body in action. Physical education provides opportunities for pupils to be creative, competitive and to face up to different challenges as individuals and in groups and teams. It promotes positive attitudes towards active and healthy lifestyles. Pupils*

learn how to think in different ways to suit a wide variety of creative, competitive and challenging activities. They learn how to plan, perform and evaluate actions, ideas and performances to improve their quality and effectiveness. Through this process pupils discover their aptitudes, abilities and preferences, and make choices about how to get involved in lifelong physical activity.

At all the key stages four areas of skill, knowledge and understanding are expected to be taught:

- acquiring and developing skills
- selecting and applying skills, tactics and compositional ideas
- evaluating and improving performance
- knowledge and understanding of fitness and health.

These skills areas are expected to be taught through a series of activities set out under the breadth of study section of the National Curriculum. At key stage 1 these are dance, games and gymnastics. For key stages 2–4 swimming, athletics and outdoor and adventurous activities are added to the list.

The attainment targets for physical education are written in broad terms. Parents will be reassured about the emphasis given to safety. At level 2, for example, pupils are expected 'to understand how to exercise safely' and the importance of this self-awareness is repeated at higher levels. In contrast to the old style 'games' that many adults remember, emphasis is also given to understanding why personal fitness and exercise is one key to a healthy life.

These issues are reflected in the descriptions of attainment for each of the eight levels set out in the National Curriculum. Levels 2 and 5 illustrate the programme of expectations between primary and secondary schooling.

Level 2

Pupils explore simple skills. They copy, remember, repeat and explore simple actions with control and co-ordination. They vary skills, actions and ideas and link these in ways that suit the activities. They begin to show some understanding of simple tactics and basic compositional ideas. They talk about differences between their own and others' performance and suggest improvements. They understand how to exercise safely, and describe how their bodies feel during different activities.

Level 5

Pupils select and combine their skills, techniques and ideas and apply them accurately and appropriately, consistently showing precision, control and fluency. When performing, they draw on what they know about strategy, tactics and composition. They analyse and comment on skills and techniques and how these are applied in their own and others' work. They modify and refine skills and techniques to improve their performance. They explain how the body reacts during different types of exercise, and warm up and cool down in ways that suit the activity. They explain why regular, safe exercise is good for their fitness and health.

There is wide scope for schools to interpret the physical education National Curriculum in different ways. The skills of the teachers involved may lead to particular activities being developed more than others. At the individual pupil level, as well, particularly as they grow older, there is scope for particular interests to be followed. The attainment targets are broadly worked and can be achieved through a wide range of physical education programmes.

Citizenship

This is a new subject introduced for the first time into the secondary National Curriculum in 2000. There have been concerns for some time that young people are insufficiently aware of their rights and responsibilities in society. A number of commissions and working parties over the last twenty years have produced reports and recommendations about this. It remains controversial whether introducing a compulsory National Curriculum specification will really impact on attitudes and behaviour. It is early days and this is likely to be one of the areas of the National Curriculum from 2000 to 2005 that comes under particular scrutiny.

The importance of citizenship is described as follows:

> *Citizenship gives pupils the knowledge, skills and understanding to play an effective role in society at local, national and international levels. It helps them to become informed, thoughtful and responsible citizens who are aware of their duties and rights. It promotes their spiritual, moral, social and cultural development, making them more self-confident and responsible both in and beyond the classroom. It encourages pupils to play a helpful part in the life of their schools, neighbourhoods, communities and the wider world. It also teaches them about our economy and democratic institutions and values; encourages respect for different national, religious and ethnic identities; and develops pupils' ability to reflect on issues and take part in discussions.*

> *Citizenship is complemented by the framework for personal, social and health education at key stages 3 and 4.*

The subject is described in terms of three areas of knowledge, skills and understanding:

- knowledge and understanding about becoming informed citizens
- developing skills of enquiry and communication
- developing skills of participation and responsible action.

Thus pupils should obtain knowledge and understanding about the importance of resolving conflict fairly and the significance of the media in society (key stage 3), as well as at key stage 4 the opportunities for individuals and voluntary groups to bring about social change locally, nationally, in Europe and internationally. Pupils at key stage 4 should also understand the importance of a free press, and the media's role in society, including the internet, in providing information and affecting opinion. Numerous other areas of citizenship are listed in the programme of study. The attainment targets are described in terms of what pupils should know and understand at the end of key stages 3 and 4:

Key stage 3

Pupils have a broad knowledge and understanding of the topical events they study; the rights, responsibilities and duties of citizens; the role of the voluntary sector; forms of government; provision of public services; and the criminal and legal systems. They show how the public gets information and how opinion is formed and expressed, including through the media. They show understanding of how and why changes take place in society. Pupils take part in school and community-based activities, demonstrating personal and group responsibility in their attitudes to themselves and others.

Key stage 4

Pupils have a comprehensive knowledge and understanding of the topical events they study; the rights, responsibilities and duties of citizens; the role of the voluntary sector; forms of government; and the criminal and civil justice, legal and economic systems. They obtain and use different kinds of information, including the media, to form and express an opinion. They evaluate the effectiveness of different ways of bringing about change at different levels of society. Pupils take part effectively in school and community-based activities, showing a willingness and commitment to evaluate such activities critically. They demonstrate personal and group responsibility in their attitudes to themselves and others.

Schools have been teaching many of these topics for many years. Personal and social education appeared, and still appears, on the curriculum of many secondary schools. This is the first time, however, that requirements have been prescribed. As with information and communication technology, schools are likely to adopt very different approaches. Some may subsume the whole or part of the requirements in relation to citizenship into existing subjects, such as history. Others may teach it as a separate subject. Individual schools will provide guidance on how the requirements are met.

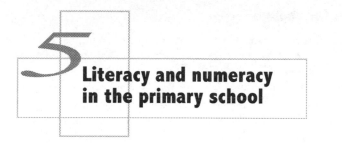

Literacy and numeracy in the primary school

In primary subjects in England, the National Curriculum programmes of study offer a basis for schools' own detailed planning. The orders for England set out the skills and knowledge pupils are expected to have acquired by the end of each key stage, without going into the detail of how this knowledge is to be incorporated into lesson planning, what teaching strategies should be adopted, or when in the course of the key stage it should be taught.

However, although the statutory position for English and mathematics is the same as that for the other National Curriculum subjects (i.e. following the programmes of study is the only legal requirement), practice in the overwhelming majority of English State primary schools is now significantly influenced by the demands of the National Literacy Strategy and the National Numeracy Strategy. Programmes of study for English and Mathematics at key stages 1 and 2 include a marginal note '...the Framework [of the National Literacy and Numeracy Strategies] provides a detailed basis for implementing the statutory requirements of the programmes of study'. The expectation that schools will follow this detailed guidance is clear, and is reflected, for example, in the approach adopted by OFSTED, who look for evidence of a whole-school strategy for raising literacy and numeracy standards (with the National Literacy and Numeracy Strategies as implicit bench-marks) in the course of regular inspections.

Context for change

The National Literacy and Numeracy Strategies were implemented in the light of concerns about the standards of literacy and numeracy achieved in schools. Results from the national end of key stage assessments in English in 1996, for example, showed only around 60% of 11 year olds to be reaching expected standards in maths and English. There is little evidence of standards declining. A major review of research on literacy by Beard (see reference section at the end of this chapter) showed that standards remained stable in the period between 1948 and 1996. However, the key issue remains – how to improve existing standards.

Some international comparative studies appeared to support the view that British education was relatively ineffective in developing skills in reading and mathematics. Neither the National Curriculum as it stood, nor the traditional pattern of schools developing their own approaches to literacy and mathematics (often with LEA guidance) were seen as delivering sufficiently high, or consistent, standards.

The National Literacy Strategy and the Labour Party's Literacy Task Force were launched by the new Labour government in Sept 1998, as a radical scheme to raise standards over the lifetime of a single parliament. The National Numeracy Strategy (based on the work of the Numeracy Task Force and the National Numeracy Project) followed a year later with similar aims and targets.

Introducing the National Strategies

Although schools had become accustomed to a high degree of central direction of their curriculum, the National Literacy Strategy broke from established practice in at least three ways:

■   it required specific steps to be taken in the area of *school development and management*;

■   it entailed a specific *professional development* programme for all primary teachers in England;

■   it dictated the adoption of specific *teaching strategies*, and methods of organising classes and their time.

School development and management

Before the introduction of each of the Strategies, schools were required to audit their current provision for teaching literacy and numeracy and produce an action plan. They were required to set targets for the number of children reaching the expected level (National Curriculum level 4) at the end of key stage 2, within the context of contributing to LEA targets and national targets of 80% and 75% for literacy and numeracy respectively. The development of medium-term plans for the implementation of each Framework was required. Schools received support from newly appointed literacy and numeracy consultants, from whom schools whose results fell furthest below expectations received intensive support. Both Strategies view the active involvement of head teachers and subject co-ordinators as essential to progress.

Professional development

The ability of primary teachers to teach literacy is by far the most important factor in whether or not children learn to read and write well. (DfEE, 1997)

Perhaps the most significant feature of the two initiatives was the acceptance that universal change could not be expected without ensuring that all teachers were in possession of the skills and subject knowledge essential to the prescribed approach to planning and teaching. Substantial training materials were developed and distributed to schools to be used on prescribed in-school training days and at subsequent staff meetings. In addition, the Numeracy Strategy set great store by giving teachers opportunities to observe consultants and other specially chosen teachers delivering demonstration lessons using the whole-class interactive approach. Both Strategies supply schools with video sequences of model lessons. Where the programmes of study had focused exclusively on the 'what' of the curriculum, the video and other resources gave teachers much greater detail of the what, the 'how', and the 'when'.

Distinctive teaching methods

The conclusions of both the Task Forces and the National Projects required an approach to teaching which represented a radical departure for many schools. Work within the National Literacy and Numeracy Strategies was to be characterised by:

- a daily lesson of specified duration dedicated exclusively to each subject
- a significant proportion of whole-class teaching in every lesson
- an emphasis on direct teaching rather than independent learning
- highly structured sessions
- a common planning Framework listing termly teaching objectives

The Numeracy Strategy has two further key principles:

- an emphasis on mental calculation
- controlled differentiation (this is a technical phrase referring to the way in which teachers should allow for individuals and groups to work to the measures of their ability, rather than just follow the average for the class).

The National Literacy Strategy Framework suggests teaching approaches and favours phonic (i.e. letter-sound based) and meaning-based approaches to reading by requiring that:

- all literacy lessons include teaching at text, sentence and word level.

The emphasis was to be on *direct teaching* with the use of *whole-class teaching* maximising pupils' direct contact with their teacher. Both frameworks also identify a role for homework in practising skills. The dedicated daily time for literacy was set at one hour, with 45 minutes at key stage 1 and 50-60 minutes at key stage 2 for mathematics.

The Literacy and Numeracy Frameworks

In order to ensure continuity and progression, each framework breaks down the requirements of the programmes of study into several hundred teaching objectives which are organised into a term by term programme for the whole of key stages 1, 2 and the reception year.

Within the Literacy Framework, each term's objectives are accompanied by a list of text types to be used in lessons. This specification ensures that the range of text types detailed in the programmes of study is covered. The Numeracy Framework distinguishes key objectives, which should be given priority in planning.

Objectives for reading and writing are organised into **three strands**:

- **text level objectives**

  At text level, children learn about how a range of fiction and non-fiction text types are constructed, acquire higher order reading skills, such as those associated with research, and learn how to evaluate the quality, effectiveness and credibility of texts. Texts shared by the whole class (either as readers or as writers) offer a context for learning at 'lower' levels.

- **sentence level objectives**

  Work at sentence level focuses on grammar and punctuation.

- **word level objectives**

  Word level work focuses on phonics in key stage 1 and spelling and vocabulary (and where necessary phonics) at key stage 2.

Although each level has specific time allocated within the Literacy Hour, the interaction between levels is acknowledged; work at sentence and word level may, for example, concentrate on structures and vocabulary typical of a particular text type or *genre*.

Teaching in the Numeracy Framework is based on *units of work*, each with its own time allocation (expressed as numbers of lessons). The

Numeracy Framework's objectives are organised into *five strands* derived from the National Curriculum:

- Number and the number system
- Calculations
- Solving problems
- Measures shape and space
- Handling data.

Both Frameworks support schools' medium term (termly or half termly) planning, which determines when particular objectives are to be taught and short term (weekly) planning, which specifies teaching methods. The Literacy Framework advocates planning for both continuous work (e.g. developing phonic knowledge) and blocked work (e.g. learning to write a persuasive text) whilst the Numeracy Framework requires continuous attention to mental calculation. Assessment is against each framework's objectives and linked to targets. The Numeracy Framework allows for the possibility of interconnecting the subject matter of different strands, provided these connections are made clear to pupils.

The Literacy Hour and the Mathematics Lesson

Each of these two lessons follows a prescribed structure.

The **Literacy Hour** comprises:

- **whole–class shared reading or writing** (15 minutes)
  Led by the teacher, the class works together on reading or writing a text.
- **whole–class word or sentence level work** (15 minutes)

This time is spent mostly on word level work at key stage 1 and on a mix of word or sentence level work (balanced over the course of the term) in key stage 2.

■ **guided group work** (20 minutes)

Children work in groups, with the majority of the class working independently. Every day the class teacher will spend this period with one (key stage 2) or two (key stage 1) groups on a **guided reading** or **guided writing** task. During guided reading, the teacher assesses and supports individuals as they read a common text. As children progress through the Framework, the emphasis of this activity moves from introductory support at key stage 1 to silent reading accompanied by individual questioning and challenging at key stage 2. Guided writing involves the teacher in teaching a group about some aspect of writing. The focus of this part of the Hour should be on teaching to meet specific objectives. Guided reading and writing prepare children for working independently. Both activities require children to be grouped according to their level of attainment.

■ a **plenary session** (10 minutes)

An opportunity for consolidation, assessment, reflection and the sharing of work, finished or in progress.

Every **Mathematics Lesson**, consists of:

■ **oral work and mental calculation** (5–10 minutes)

Aimed at sharpening and rehearsing pupils' skills, sometimes focusing on those which will be needed in the main part of the lesson.

■ the **main teaching activity** (30-40 minutes)

The teacher's input and pupil activities. During this time children may be taught, or work independently, as a whole class, in groups, in pairs or even as individuals.

■ a **plenary session** (10-15 minutes)

With a similar function to that of the Literacy Hour. It is also a time for making links with pupils' use of mathematics in other subjects.

Timings for the Mathematics Lesson are more flexible than for the Literacy Hour, as, for example, an introductory lesson may need a substantial teaching input, whilst a lesson later in the week may need only a short introduction but benefit from a longer plenary. The exact proportion of time given to whole-class, group and individual work is not prescribed, though the importance of whole-class teaching is emphasised.

Developments

The National Literacy and Numeracy Strategies have continued to develop since their introduction. Literacy and numeracy consultants continue to support schools as they work towards meeting their targets and nationally planned training continues. Additional guidance on many themes, including mixed year classes, small schools, more able children, children of reception age, children with English as an additional language, children with special educational needs has been issued by the Government. In the latter two cases the guidance emphasises the Strategies' principle that all children should be included within all the parts of the Literacy hour. The *progression in phonics* materials help enliven whole-class teaching in key stage 1.

As schools have grown more confident in their deployment of the elements of the strategy, some flexibility has developed within the structure of the Literacy Hour; the original format as defined by the 'Literacy Hour Clock' is often modified, though the basic teaching strategies should continue to be employed and, most importantly, the objectives must remain at the heart of planning and assessment.

Practical initiatives aimed at raising achievement include:

■ **Additional Literacy Support** (ALS)

a programme, designed to support those children entering key stage 2 without having fully mastered the word level objectives for key stage 1;

■ **Springboard 5**

a mathematics programme for Year 5 children at risk of not attaining level 4 by the end of key stage 2.

In many schools teaching assistants play a major role in the implementation of these programmes and DfEE training for new teaching assistants includes a significant emphasis on the Strategies.

Most of the DfEE publications regarding the National Literacy and Numeracy Strategies are available on-line on the Standards site: http://www.standards.dfee.gov.uk/ where teachers will also find study support materials to develop their own subject knowledge. Professional development is also supported by publications from the Qualifications and Curriculum Authority (QCA).

Useful references relating to primary Literacy and Numeracy Strategies

Beard, R (1998) *National Literacy Strategy: review of research and other related evidence*

DfEE (1997) *The implementation of the National Literacy Strategy (final report of the Literacy Task Force)*

DfEE (1998a) *The National Literacy Strategy Framework for Teaching Mathematics from Reception to Year 6*

DfEE (1998b) *Numeracy Matters: the preliminary report of the Numeracy Task Force*

DfEE (1998c) *Teaching: High Status, High Standards*

DfEE (1999) *The National Numeracy Strategy Framework for Teaching*

Mullis, I V S, Martin, M O, Beaton, A E, Gonzales, E J, Kelly, D L and Smith, T A (1997) *Mathematics Achievement in the Primary School Years: IEA's Third International Mathematics and Science Study (TIMMS)*, Centre for the study of testing, evaluation and educational policy, Boston College, Chestnut Hill, MA.

OFSTED (1998) *The National Literacy Project: HMI Evaluation*

OFSTED (1999a), *The National Literacy Strategy: an evaluation of the first year of the National Literacy Strategy*

OFSTED (1999b) *National Numeracy Project: HMI Evaluation*

OFSTED (1999c) *National Numeracy Strategy: An Interim Evaluation*

OFSTED (2000a) *National Literacy Strategy: the second year*

OFSTED (2000b) *National Numeracy Strategy: the first year*

QCA (1999) *The National Curriculum: handbook for primary teachers in England*

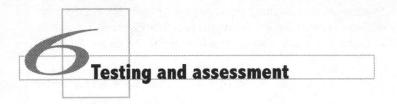

Testing and assessment

Testing and assessment is the issue that produces the greatest controversy amongst educationists, parents, and the general public. For pupils and parents, it can be one of the most worrying aspects of school life. It is also, ultimately, one of the most important. Examination success is a significant factor in determining job prospects or access to further or higher education. If you want to be a vet, the very highest grades at Advanced (A) Level are required. You need A levels, too, to begin university training as a primary school teacher but, in addition, you must also achieve General Certificates of Secondary Education (GCSE) grades A-C in English, mathematics and science.

The National Curriculum is accompanied by statutory assessment in the form of national tests at the end of each key stage. These take the form of General Certificate of Secondary Education (GCSE) examinations at the end of key stage 4. Before the National Curriculum, most pupils, apart from taking reading tests, were well into secondary school before they came into contact with a nationally standardised examination. Now a measurement of pupil achievement in core subjects is made at each key stage. Young children are also assessed at the point they enter formal schooling. This is called a baseline assessment, which gives teachers and parents a marker or bench-mark against which subsequent progress can be made. Many parents support this idea. This is not surprising, as most parents expect some sort of feedback about how well their children are doing. Though some parents have raised concerns about the stress that some children feel, linked to the extent of national testing.

Measuring achievement, however, is not a straightforward process and the Government has spent millions of pounds on research projects in attempting to produce fair and reliable ways of testing children. It is further complicated because national testing is designed to serve many different purposes. The National Curriculum 2000-2005 identifies as one of its key purposes establishing national standards for the performance of all pupils in all subjects. The standards are explicitly set out so that they can be used to set targets, measure progress towards targets and compare performance between individuals, groups and schools. The results of national tests can, therefore, be used to make a judgement about an individual child against national expectations of attainment; compare an individual child with others in their class or with a national average; compare schools across the country; and monitor a teacher's or a school's or a Local Education Authority's (LEA's) effectiveness in raising standards – particularly in mathematics and English. It is difficult to design simple tests that can be used reliably to meet all these purposes. This lies at the heart of much of the controversy over testing.

This 'high stakes' type of assessment, where the result has an impact on a child's or teacher's or school's prospects and is made public, isn't the only type of assessment. Teachers will use a variety of assessment strategies on a day-to-day basis in order to monitor children's progress, diagnose difficulties, set targets for further achievement and plan future lessons. Children, too, may be involved in assessment, through assessing each other's work (peer assessment) or their own work (self assessment). Though less controversial, most teachers and parents would agree that these teacher assessments are most important in the daily business of helping children learn.

The remainder of this chapter will look at testing and assessment in more detail, explain the purposes, types and methods, and explore further the controversial issues.

But, first, as you can see from the opening paragraphs, assessment is full of jargon and we need to define some terms.

First, is there a difference between the terms 'assessment', 'examination', 'tests' and 'national tests'? The answer is no and all four terms can be used interchangeably. However, in practice, some distinctions are generally made in schools today.

Assessment is generally a broad term used to cover tests, examinations and all the ways in which teachers check and monitor children's learning and measure progress and achievement. *Examinations* tend to refer to external public examinations, such as GCSE or A level, although some schools, almost exclusively at secondary level, have end-of-year internal examinations for some or all year groups not taking public examinations. *Tests* describe short, usually written, assessments set and marked by teachers to see how well an individual, group or class has learned over a period of time or on a particular topic. Internal assessments, like these, help teachers to plan future work and activities for individuals and for classes as a whole. *National tests* are tests marked outside the school and normally taken at ages, 7, 11 and 14 in the core subjects of English, mathematics and science. These provide information on overall achievement in these subjects at the end of a key stage.

Approaches to assessment

The sort of assessment that merely gives you a grade (in a public examination for example) tells you very little about which parts of the syllabus you did well in or where you went wrong. Giving you a position on a class list is much the same: all you can tell from the list is how you compare to others. More recent developments in assessment attempt to be more informative.

1   The assessment process attempts to recognise when children have achieved a target, to acknowledge this in a positive way, and then to help the teacher to plan the next step for learning. This is called *formative* assessment.

2   The assessment process aims to reveal weaknesses or difficulties in such a way that appropriate help can be given and the child can overcome the learning problem. This is termed the *diagnostic* purpose of assessment. This reflects the way that most people learn. Initially, learners experience patchy understanding. It is important to spot areas of weakness and remedy them through extra work and attention. The

driving-test, for example, tries to be diagnostic. You are given feedback on the specific parts of the test that you fail. As you trek back sadly to your instructor for further lessons, and additional expense, it would serve little purpose to say that you had a D fail grade! The detailed feedback that you receive will help to focus both your learning and your instructor's teaching before retaking the test.

The process of continually making and recording these assessment judgements on progress should, if working well, provide important formative and diagnostic information on every child. It is worth emphasising that the aim is *to show children what they have achieved*, not where they have failed.

3   The assessment process aims to give teachers, the child and parents an overall summary of what has been achieved, at regular intervals. This is called *summative* assessment. In the National Curriculum subjects, the summary is made on the basis of achievement against the eight levels in the attainment targets, up to the age of 14. The eight level descriptions show increasing difficulty from level 1 to level 8 with a further description for *exceptional performance* above level 8.

4   The results of national tests and public examinations are used by teachers, headteachers, governors and parents to see how well the school is doing against set targets. LEAs and Government, similarly use these national assessments to check progress against Government targets (in mathematics and English). This is called the *evaluative* purpose of assessment. Using national assessment information to make comparisons between schools has led to great controversy.

The results of national tests at each key stage and public examinations are recorded for each school and published in national 'league tables'. There has been much criticism of this. Not least, because where a school appears in the league tables can have an impact on parental choice and pupil enrolment. Schools, generally, do not object to publication of national assessment results *per se* but they do object when the type of data published does not allow fair comparisons to be made. Schools situated in socially and economically advantaged areas almost always achieve better results than schools in an urban, deprived environment. To counter this, a number of ways of showing the progress that children make within a school (termed 'value added'), from one key stage to the next, to place alongside the outcome of national tests and examinations, are being developed. The 'value-added' dimension has become increasingly important in comparing schools, especially since 'value-added' league tables often show schools in socially deprived areas doing very well in comparison to more favourably situated schools. The Government has accepted this argument and is committed to producing more sophisticated tables of results. There is, at least theoretically, the possibility that 'value-added' assessment could be made at the end of key stage 1 now that all children are given a 'baseline' assessment soon after starting their first year of school.

Most important, schools now have access to rich national and local information on national tests and examinations, which allows them to compare their results with other schools or groups of schools *that have similar characteristics*. Schools and individual teachers now regularly use this 'bench-marking' information to set realistic targets for improvement and to check progress. This evaluative purpose of assessment is gaining importance and teachers are enthusiastic about how this can help them improve pupil learning.

All teachers now use assessment for diagnostic and formative purposes. This is, of course, nothing new. The best teachers have always used this approach. The National Curriculum gives it added impetus and, in particular, offers the chance to make assessment a positive experience for the child. A further distinction, between norm-reference assessment and criterion-referenced assessment helps to explain this more clearly.

The old system of assessment was almost wholly *norm-referenced*. That is, pupils were placed in rank order and predetermined proportions of students would be allocated certain grades. *Norm-referenced* grades are assigned by comparing the performance of one child with another, rather than assigning a grade based on the quality of an individual child's performance against set criteria. The idea about pre-determined proportions was considered in Chapter 2. The 'bell curve' was, and in some cases still is, used to allocate grades. Take the 11-plus examination for example, still used in parts of the country to allocate places at grammar schools. Places in these schools are fixed and 'pass' grades are limited to match the number of places available. No matter how well a particular child performs on the test, if others who are ranked above him or her have filled the places, the (s)he cannot be admitted.

The great difficulty with norm-referencing is that a proportion of students are, inevitably, deemed to have done badly and come away with a negative experience, not only of the examination or test but of school generally. The alternative to norm-referencing is termed *criterion-referencing*. The National Curriculum assessment system is an attempt to move towards criterion-referencing. Criterion-referenced assessment means that a child's achievements are judged in relation to specific objectives, irrespective of other children's performance. The Driving Test is a good example of criterion-referenced assessment. Success or failure doesn't depend on how others taking the test have performed. The examiner isn't limited to passing only 50% of those taking it, no matter how well they performed. Success depends on your ability to show that you meet pre-determined criteria. If the 11-plus examination were criterion-referenced then specific assessment criteria for entry would have to be agreed. This means additional places at grammar schools would have to be created in 'good' years or withdrawn if a particular cohort was unable to meet the entry criteria.

Categories of assessment

Continuous assessment is on-going assessment carried out by teachers. It is the daily and weekly record of assessments on all aspects of the curriculum organised by teachers. Information from written work, from children's answers to questions, from the way that they perform practical tasks, either on their own or in a group, is transferred onto a child's personal record. Every so often a teacher will review all this information and make a judgement about the level of work being achieved. Teachers do this by judging which of the National Curriculum level descriptions for a subject best matches the child's performance. At the end of a key stage, teachers will draw on a wide variety of different assessments carried out across a long period of time to record their final judgement on the National Curriculum level achieved. This is called the *teacher assessment* and is reported to parents alongside the national test result in the same subject. Teachers usually keep some of the children's work as evidence to support the teacher assessment.

National Tests are written and set outside the school by organisations commissioned by the QCA (Qualifications and Curriculum Authority). Towards the end of a key stage, children will complete a number of activities that will be marked and recorded to measure their level of attainment in the core subjects (English, mathematics and science).

These national tests serve three purposes. Firstly, in combination with the teacher assessment, they are reported to parents in an end-of-year report. Both show which level on the 8 point scale the child has reached. This enables parents to see their child's progress and to make broad comparisons with the average attainment achieved in the school, locally and nationally. Secondly, by comparing the levels reached by children on these national tests with the judgements made by teachers through the continuous assessment process, it is possible to check that teacher assessments are in line with nationally agreed standards. Of course, it needs to be remembered that national tests are designed to be straightforward to administer and mark externally and are not designed to assess the full range of knowledge, skills and understanding. This is only possible through continuous assessment by teachers. This is why teacher assessment and national test results are of equal standing when teachers report on pupils' progress. Thirdly, the results are collated and reported in different forms to enable comparisons to be made and targets for improvement to be set. Examples of this, we have already explained, are national 'league tables' and bench-marking information.

How continuous assessment works

Teachers are unable to assess all the children in their class all the time. Throughout the year, therefore, it is likely that, in any one lesson, they will give particular attention to two or three children, or a particular group. The teacher could on one day:

- as part of the Literacy Hour, have individual conversations during guided writing with members of one group to see if they could briefly describe an event from the previous day. The teacher will be experienced in judging whether the child is confident in doing this or whether further practice is needed (in which case the teacher might plan an activity in the group where the child can take practice further). The teacher would also make a mental (or perhaps written) note to have another conversation later in the week in which an event can be described briefly.

- after school, spend some time looking at the written work completed by all the children. The teacher would be looking, for example, for evidence of sentences with appropriate use of grammar such as consistent use of capital letters, full stops and question marks – the choice, will, of course, be influenced by current objectives and targets. As (s)he looked at the books the teacher would make a note against each child's record. It is unlikely that a judgement would be made about whether a child would be fully competent on the basis of one piece of written work. The teacher will build up knowledge of each child over the year and will use a variety of evidence in making a final teacher assessment.

  A secondary science teacher working on rocks and soil will be involved in a similar process.

- In this class, the teacher is using a recording system that allows him or her to note when pupils are successful with practical activities. In science classes, pupils would not normally all do the same activity, then stop and wait to have their worked marked by the teacher. More commonly they carry out investigations and the teacher observes different parts of the process to see how well they are doing. During a number of lessons, therefore, the teacher will observe all the groups and make judgements about the individuals' progress.

■   In the same class, the teacher may set a written assignment, following reading and discussion in class, that provides evidence of the pupils' understanding of different weathering processes. The teacher's written comments in the pupils' workbooks would indicate how well they had done by commenting on their knowledge and understanding. The teacher might also suggest how the work could be improved, extended or might suggest different work to ensure a better understanding of the concept. Depending on the results, the teacher could decide: (1) to do something with the whole class on this concept; (2) to follow up the concept with a group; or (3) to give some individual help as the vast majority had clearly demonstrated their understanding.

Teachers throughout the year, as we have explained earlier in this chapter, use continuous assessment. It requires careful systems for recording assessment for individuals, groups and classes. It forms the basis for deciding a pupil's level of achievement in each subject and is reported, as teacher assessment, to parents each year in the school report.

The national tests

This was an area of major national controversy when the National Curriculum was first implemented. Teachers complained that the tests were too time-consuming and disrupted the normal curriculum. Teachers and parents were worried about the fairness of the actual tests used and continue to be concerned about some inconsistencies in the way that tests marked by external examiners at key stages 2 and 3 are graded. All of those concerned were worried about the way that the tests were reported in a 'league-table' format, providing a pecking order of schools. Publishing national test results has also been blamed for the emphasis on the core subjects above all other areas of the curriculum, leading for example to a reduction in creative arts in schools.

There have been major changes to national testing in the last decade. Most importantly, national tests were slimmed down and the role and standing of teacher assessment was given greater importance. Both now have equal standing. There may however, be variations in the levels reported between them because the simplified national tests cannot cover everything the teacher assessment does.

A summary of the testing and reporting arrangements is outlined below:

Key stage 1

At key stage 1 there are national tests in English and mathematics. In English, pupils are assessed in reading, writing (including handwriting) and spelling. Children take one test in mathematics. Teacher assessment takes place in English, mathematics and science. The majority of pupils are expected to work within levels 1-3. The majority of pupils are expected to attain level 2 at age 7.

Key stage 2

At the end of key stage 2, children are tested in English, mathematics and science. In English, this includes tests in reading, writing (including handwriting) and spelling. Mathematics includes the testing of mental arithmetic as well as a written test. There are teacher assessments in English, mathematics and science. The majority of pupils are expected to work between levels 2–5. The majority of pupils are expected to attain level 4 at age 11.

Key stage 3

At the end of key stage 3, pupils are tested in English (including reading, writing, and studying a Shakespeare play), mathematics (including mental arithmetic) and science. In the non-core foundation subjects of history, geography, a modern foreign language, design and technology, information technology, art, music and RE, teachers report a teacher assessment. They do this by considering the continuous assessments carried out over a period of time and matching these to one of the eight level descriptions or the description for exceptional performance. In schools, this sort of broad-brush assessment is called 'best fit'. The majority of pupils are expected to work between levels 3-7 in key stage 3. The majority of pupils are expected to attain level 5/6 at age 14.

Key stage 4

At key stage 4, national qualifications form the basis for assessment. Pupils may follow courses leading to a number of qualifications: GCSE; GCSE (short course); GNVQ at foundation, intermediate and advanced level.

There are tests that 8-, 9- and 10-year-old pupils can take between Key Stage 1 and Key Stage 2, but these are not compulsory and are not reported. Some schools use them because they find them helpful in checking pupils' progress annually and to give extra practice in taking tests. Others have criticised this as being another example of the narrowing of the curriculum and 'teaching to the test'.

Reporting to parents

Schools report each pupil's progress in all of the National Curriculum subjects on an annual basis. Schools may report on progress towards a particular level description or indicate which level the pupil is currently working within. At the end of a key stage a school reports both teacher assessments on the levels achieved in each subject and the outcome of national tests, where appropriate. At ages 7 and 11 schools may give 'age standardised' scores to parents. These scores will tell them how well their child has done compared with others born at the same time. The reports will also tell them how their child is getting on in other areas, such as personal and social education and their attendance for the year. Information is also included on what to do if the parents want to discuss the report in more detail.

The legal necessity to report to parents annually in all National Curriculum subjects and report on national test results at the end of each key stage, although extremely important, only represent one part of the school curriculum. Achievement in other areas, recognised and recorded through *records of achievement* provide a more balanced view of pupils' achievements in all areas of their lives.

Alongside teachers' continuous assessment, national tests and public examinations, this development has had a major impact. *Records of achievement* were first planned in the 1970s and early 1980s to give much greater acknowledgement to what young people achieved in school. Originally, this began in secondary schools, where the vast majority of school leavers had very little to show for their efforts and enthusiasm across the broad range of school life. Examination results gave an indication of academic attainment, but what about all the other qualities that schools have a responsibility to develop?

Achievements in creative activities, the school play or other aspects of drama, music and dance gained little recognition. Sporting achievement may have gained passing recognition as well as the whole host of pursuits that a good school fosters: outdoor activities; community help programmes; charity fund-raising events, to name but a few. But there was no on-going record that the pupils could take away with them that recorded these successes. Only a very few schools systematically recorded a pupil's wider achievements.

By the late 1980s, a great many schools were using a 'record of achievement'. The form and style varied from area to area but most aimed to record achievements in all aspects of school life and important achievements outside school.

Now, all children leave school with a national record of achievement. Pupils work with a form tutor or counsellor to record, compile and collate records that provide information about a whole host of achievements. This record contains information about academic work as well, including grades obtained in public examinations. It is not only the final grade that counts though, and this document recognises a pupil's achievements on the journey to examination success.

Many young people choose to use their record of achievement at interviews with potential employers or when transferring to other forms of education. It is also a document to be kept at home, treasured and years later shown with some pride to the grandchildren!

The Future

The public and political controversies that were associated with testing in the early 1990s have now given way to a degree of consensus. Teachers accept that parents want some measure of individual, school and national progress. Governments have accepted that it is too costly and time-consuming to test in every subject at every key stage. Parents have a statutory right to receive annual reports on their child's progress against the level descriptions in each National Curriculum subject. Teacher continuous assessments form the basis of the annual reports. National tests, after some early expensive failures, have been developed into a simpler form, focusing on core subjects only at the end of each key stage.

The most likely area of development in the early years of the 21st Century is in the sophisticated use of national assessment data. With more information and communications technologies available, schools can use local and national assessment to set their own targets for improvement and teachers to monitor more effectively individual pupil progress. Parents are likely to see greater use of target setting against performance criteria for individual children, not only in National Curriculum subjects but also in the wider school curriculum, such as personal and social education. The public is likely to see greater use of 'value-added' information to make comparisons between schools in national published 'league tables' more fair. The closer links, particularly in key stage 4 and beyond, between vocational and academic courses, are likely to continue to affect the range of national qualifications available for pupils to demonstrate their achievements and success.

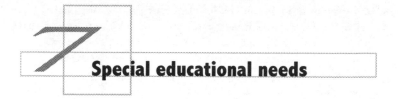

Special educational needs

Many people are now aware that the school provision for children with special educational needs (SEN) underwent revolutionary changes in the 1980s and 1990s. The initial impetus came from a report on the education of 'handicapped children and young people' published in 1978 (The Warnock Report). This established clearly that educational goals should be the same for all young people, regardless of any disabilities they might have. In 1981, an Education Act was passed, and in the following decade, children with SEN who had been educated separately were gradually integrated into mainstream schools. An influential Green Paper, *'Excellence for all children – meeting special educational needs'*, was published in 1997. In the following year, the DfEE published *'Meeting special educational needs – a programme of action'* which outlined the action that was planned to develop good practice in the organisation and provision of special educational needs across Britain.

The revision of the National Curriculum in 2000 established 'inclusion', rather than 'integration', as a fundamental principle. The significant difference between the two terms is that integration can be interpreted as merely accommodating pupils with SEN in a mainstream setting whilst inclusion implies that the institution will need to adapt to ensure total access to the education and social opportunities on offer. A small minority of children will always need the specialist teaching and resources that a special school can offer. However, many LEAs are now developing their special schools as community special schools with a role to develop outreach services, increase integration activities and share their expertise across the educational community.

The principles of inclusion are now laid down in the National Curriculum. All teachers have a statutory responsibility to ensure that all pupils are effectively included in their classrooms. The revised National Curriculum has considerably more flexibility than its predecessor and it is anticipated that all pupils, including those with the most complex needs in special schools, will be able to access the full National Curriculum without the school having to arrange for disapplication, the formal term used when any child is deemed unable to study all or part of the National Curriculum. In extreme and increasingly rare circumstances, schools can still arrange for a child to be disapplied from aspects of the Curriculum. Schools can also request that special arrangements, such as extra time, are made available for pupils with SEN who are sitting national tests or public examinations.

The three principles for inclusion from the National Curriculum are set out below.

A   Setting suitable learning challenges

1   Teachers should aim to give every pupil the opportunity to experience success in learning and to achieve as high a standard as possible. The National Curriculum programmes of study set out what most pupils should be taught at each key stage – but teachers should teach the knowledge, skills and understanding in ways that suit their pupils' abilities. This may mean choosing knowledge, skills and understanding from earlier or later key stages so that individual pupils can make progress and show what they can achieve. Where it is appropriate for pupils to make extensive use of content from an earlier key stage, there may not be time to teach all aspects of the age-related programmes of study. A similarly flexible approach will be needed to take account of any gaps in pupils' learning resulting from missed or interrupted schooling.

2   For pupils whose attainments fall significantly below the expected levels at a particular key stage, a much greater degree of differentiation will be necessary. In these circumstances,

teachers may need to use the content of the programmes of study as a resource or to provide a context in planning learning appropriate to the age and requirements of their pupils.

3   For pupils whose attainments significantly exceed the expected level of attainment within one or more subjects during a particular key stage, teachers will need to plan suitably challenging work. As well as drawing on materials from later key stages or higher levels of study, teachers may plan further differentiation by extending the breadth and depth of study within individual subjects or by planning work which draws on the content of different subjects.

B   Responding to pupils' diverse learning needs

1   When planning, teachers should set high expectations and provide opportunities for all pupils to achieve, including boys and girls, pupils with special educational needs, pupils with disabilities, pupils from all social and cultural backgrounds, pupils of different ethnic groups including travellers, refugees and asylum seekers, and those from diverse linguistic backgrounds. Teachers need to be aware that pupils bring to school different experiences, interests and strengths which will influence the way in which they learn. Teachers should plan their approaches to teaching and learning so that all pupils can take part in lessons fully and effectively.

2   To ensure that they meet the full range of pupils' needs, teachers should be aware of the requirements of the equal opportunities legislation that covers race, gender and disability.

3   Teachers should take specific action to respond to pupils' diverse needs by:

   (a)   creating effective learning environments

   (b)   securing their motivation and concentration

   (c)   providing equality of opportunity through teaching approaches

(d) using appropriate assessment approaches

(e) setting targets for learning.

C Overcoming potential barriers to learning and assessment for individuals and groups of pupils

A minority of pupils will have particular learning and assessment requirements which go beyond the provisions described in sections A and B and, if not addressed, could create barriers to learning. These requirements are likely to arise as a consequence of a pupil having a special educational need or disability or may be linked to a pupil's progress in learning English as an additional language.

1   Teachers must take account of these requirements and make provision, where necessary, to support individuals or groups of pupils to enable them to participate effectively in the curriculum and assessment activities. During end-of-key-stage assessments, teachers should bear in mind that special arrangements are available to support individual pupils.

Pupils with special educational needs

2   Curriculum planning and assessment for pupils with special educational needs must take account of the type and extent of the difficulty experienced by the pupil. Teachers will encounter a wide range of pupils with special educational needs, some of whom will also have disabilities (see paragraphs C/4 and C/5 below). In many cases, the action necessary to respond to an individual's requirements for curriculum access will be met through greater differentiation of tasks and materials, consistent with school-based intervention as set out in the SEN Code of Practice. A smaller number of pupils may need access to specialist equipment and approaches or to alternative or adapted activities, consistent with school-based intervention augmented by advice and support from external specialists as described in the SEN Code of Practice, or, in exceptional circumstances, with a statement of special educational need. Teachers should, where appropriate, work

closely with representatives of other agencies who may be supporting the pupil.

3   Teachers should take specific action to provide access to learning for pupils with special educational needs by:

(a) providing for pupils who need help with communication, language and literacy

(b) planning, where necessary, to develop pupils' understanding through the use of all available senses and experiences

(c) planning for pupils' full participation in learning and in physical and practical activities

(d) helping pupils to manage their behaviour, to take part in learning effectively and safely, and, at key stage 4, to prepare for work

(e) helping individuals to manage their emotions, particularly trauma or stress, and to take part in learning.

Pupils with disabilities

4   Not all pupils with disabilities will necessarily have special educational needs. Many pupils with disabilities learn alongside their peers with little need for additional resources beyond the aids which they use as part of their daily life, such as a wheelchair, a hearing aid or equipment to aid vision. Teachers must take action, however, in their planning to ensure that these pupils are enabled to participate as fully and effectively as possible within the National Curriculum and the statutory assessment arrangements. Potential areas of difficulty should be identified and addressed at the outset of work, without recourse to the formal provisions for disapplication.

5   Teachers should take specific action to enable the effective participation of pupils with disabilities by:

(a) planning appropriate amounts of time to allow for the satisfactory completion of tasks

(b) planning opportunities, where necessary, for the

development of skills in practical aspects of the curriculum

(c) identifying aspects of programmes of study and attainment targets that may present specific difficulties for individuals.

Pupils who are learning English as an additional language

6   Pupils for whom English is an additional language have diverse needs in terms of support necessary in English language learning. Planning should take account of such factors as the pupil's age, length of time in this country, previous educational experience and skills in other languages. Careful monitoring of each pupil's progress in the acquisition of English language skills and of subject knowledge and understanding will be necessary to confirm that no learning difficulties are present.

7   The ability of pupils for whom English is an additional language to take part in the National Curriculum may be ahead of their communication skills in English. Teachers should plan learning opportunities to help pupils develop their English and should aim to provide the support pupils need to take part in all subject areas.

8   Teachers should take specific action to help pupils who are learning English as an additional language by:

(a) developing their spoken and written English

(b) ensuring access to the curriculum and to assessment.

All schools now have a DfEE publication '*The Index for Inclusion*'. It offers guidance to schools on how to conduct a whole school audit on inclusion. The intention is that having identified ways in which the school is not fully inclusive, appropriate action can be taken to develop good practice.

In 1993, '*The Code of Practice for the Identification and Assessment of Pupils with Special Educational Needs*', usually just referred to as

The Code of Practice, was published. It described best practice in the organisation of special educational needs (SEN) provision. Some sections of the Code of Practice (those printed in royal blue bold print) are statutory.

The Code of Practice requires all schools to have policies in place which detail their arrangements for SEN provision. Parents can ask to see these policies. All schools have to maintain a register of pupils with SEN. The register should clearly show the pupil's prime need. It is also a statutory requirement for all schools to identify a teacher who will co-ordinate SEN arrangements (usually known as the SENCo) and a governor who will take a particular interest in SEN. Each year, schools must describe SEN provision in their prospectus and report on the success of their SEN policy in the Governors' Annual Report to Parents.

The Code of Practice guides schools on how to record a pupil's needs and on the development of individual education plans (IEPs). IEPs should be drawn up by a teacher designated as having responsibility for that pupil, in collaboration with the parents/carers and, where appropriate, the pupil themselves. They should clearly identify the pupil's needs and suggest targets and strategies to enable progress. IEPs typically contain around three targets. Typically, these will relate to basic literacy and numeracy but they may also include targets for improved behaviour or for the development of social and learning skills. The 1993 Code of Practice identified five stages of need, from stage one which is an initial logging of concern to stage five, when a pupil's needs would be detailed in a statement. The Code of Practice, despite its length and degree of detail, was widely welcomed by educational professionals and parents. In the years since 1993, it has made a real difference to the quality of SEN provision and practice in schools.

The Code of Practice was revised during 2000/2001. The revised Code is designed to be clearer and to reduce unnecessary bureaucracy in schools. The previous five stages have been reduced to three broad descriptors. 'school action' means that schools must act to ensure that appropriate teaching methods, activities and resources are used to enable a pupil to progress. 'school action plus' means that the SENCo has identified that further professional advice is needed. The third descriptor refers to a statement of special educational need. Schools and Local Education Authorities should be consulted for up-to-date information and advice.

A statement of special educational need is arranged for those children who experience consistent and particular difficulties which may require additional resources or professional expertise from outside the school. With the agreement and full involvement of parents throughout the process, this is drawn up by a group of professionals from a variety of backgrounds (educational psychologists, doctors, social workers and teachers). Schools are required to follow the recommendations made in the statement. Each year, the statement is reviewed. Decisions are made regarding whether the statement is still necessary and what new targets, strategies and resources should be included.

In recent years, there has been a marked shift not only towards the teaching of children with special educational needs in mainstream schools, but also teaching them in ordinary classes. Although some specialist intervention activities in groups withdrawn from the child's own class may sometimes be appropriate, teachers are now encouraged to make all of the necessary arrangements and adaptations to ensure that children can be taught alongside their peers in ordinary classes. Professional assistants (variously known as teaching assistants or learning support assistants) are present in many classes, especially in primary schools. Their role is to work in collaboration with the teacher and they are often deployed to offer specific support to pupils with special educational needs. Most Local Education Authorities offer training opportunities to teaching assistants and many are encouraged to work towards professional qualifications.

Teachers, governors and parents should consider carefully the sorts of issues that inform the development of the school's special educational needs policy. The Code of Practice outlines what a good policy statement should include. One of the first national documents following the 1993 Act (*A Curriculum for All*) is still amongst the clearest on this issue. In *A Curriculum for All*, schools were asked to develop responses to a number of questions. Examples included:

- Can the tasks and activities for any one attainment level be chosen and presented to enable children with a wide range of attainments to experience success? For instance, emphasis on oral rather than written work will help some pupils with learning difficulties.

- Can activities be matched to pupils' differing paces and styles of learning, interests, capabilities, and previous experience; can time and order of priority be allocated accordingly?

- Can the activities be broken down into a series of small and achievable steps for pupils who have marked learning difficulties?

- Will the activities stretch pupils of whom too little may have been expected in the past? These pupils are likely to include some with physical, sensory, or other impairment who are high attainers.

- Can a range of communication methods be used with pupils with language difficulties?

- Will the purpose of the activities and the means of achieving them be understood and welcomed by pupils with learning difficulties?

The school environment plays an important role in developing the learning of all pupils, but it is especially important for children with special educational needs. The layout of the classroom, the capacity to change the way pupils are grouped, the provision of information technology and other resources, and the encouragement of co-operative approaches to learning amongst pupils can all support the integration of children with special educational needs into the curriculum, and stimulate their capacity to learn.

The advice in *A Curriculum for All* gives numerous ideas and examples of how subject-teaching in the National Curriculum can be sensitive to children with special educational needs. For example,

- *Use of language*: 'Without water human beings are unable to survive' could become 'People need water to live'.

- *Practical activities*: Pupils may be given paper for folding into a windmill shape. Those with learning difficulties might need to have the shape printed on the sheet with the folds marked. For a visually impaired pupil the lines can be indented in the paper with pressure from a ball pen or a spur-wheel available from the Royal National Institute for the Blind (RNIB). This creates an embossed shape on the reverse side of the paper which the pupil can feel. Even with extra help like this, pupils will still need close guidance by the class teacher and classroom helpers.

- *Classroom method*: Teachers will need to find ways to help those pupils who have specific learning difficulties in reading and writing to make use of their oral strengths (for example, use of a tape-recorder and word-processor) and to ensure that evaluation and feedback on work are not over-dominated by hand-written products.

It is important that everyone involved, professionals, parents and governors, be fully aware of the statutory responsibilities and regulations in formulating and developing policies. The Qualifications and Curriculum Authority (QCA) offers guidance to schools on assessment, target setting, interpretation of the Curriculum, specific flexibility at Key Stage 4 and special arrangements. Local Education Authorities (LEAs) have officers and advisers who monitor the delivery of the National Curriculum and the provision that is made for pupils with special educational needs. They are also available to advise and support school staff and parents. LEAs also employ specialist teachers who have expertise in particular aspects of SEN. Many LEAs have an officer with specific responsibility for advising and supporting parents on SEN issues. OFSTED address provision for pupils with special educational needs in their inspections and also now have a specific brief to evaluate the extent to which schools successfully include all pupils.

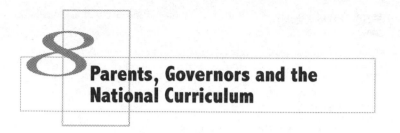

Parents, Governors and the National Curriculum

Parents are entitled to a range of information about the school curriculum in general and the progress their child is making through that curriculum. Schools are required to publish an up-to-date prospectus every year and this must contain the essential information that parents and their children would need to know. This would include a statement of the schools aims, the way the curriculum is organised and information about the school's national test and external examination results. Schools must show how the results relate to national averages. Regulations and guidance to schools on the information that must be made available to parents are published by the DfEE. This is changed from time to time and reference should be made to the DfEE web site (see the further information section) for the latest information. In Northern Ireland and Wales local regulations and guidance will exist in this area.

Parents are also entitled to an annual report on their child's progress. This will include information

- on progress in the National Curriculum subjects and other subjects and activities which are part of the school curriculum;

- on progress generally in all aspects of school life, including attendance;

- on what to do if they want to discuss the report (most schools organise interviews with parents to coincide with the publication of the report).

At the end of key stages 1, 2 and 3 the annual report will also include information on:

- the results of the national tests
- the level a pupil achieves in each part of the subject tests (for example, the levels achieved in the reading and writing parts of English)
- teachers' assessments of a pupil's progress
- for children with special educational needs the extent of the achievement in reaching a particular level in a subject.

Overall the national guidance on the reporting process says that parents should expect to have set out what their child has learned, the things they are good at and when they might need some extra help. Reports may also give parents practical guidance about how they might help their child's future progress.

In recent years, schools have become very efficient in the way this new curriculum and assessment information is published. Reporting to parents is strictly scrutinised. Parents with concerns should contact form teachers or head teachers in the first instance. Local Education Authorities also provide guidance. It would only be in the rarest of circumstances that parents might resort to a complaints procedure. These do, however, exist and information about the process involved is published in school prospectuses.

Governors

Governors share with the head teacher and the Local Education Authority the responsibility to ensure that the National Curriculum is taught and for carrying out assessments. This responsibility includes making sure that enough lesson time is provided for pupils to cover the National Curriculum and any other statutory requirements. Guidance on this is given by the DfEE and all head teachers will be aware of the recommended minimum weekly lesson times. In secondary schools the governing body must ensure that only approved external qualifications and syllabuses are offered to pupils of compulsory school age. A circular listing these is available in schools and on the DfEE web site.

The governing body are also responsible for ensuring that the head teacher fulfils all the requirements for assessing pupils and forwarding the necessary information to the Local Education Authority.

From 2000 onwards a governing body must produce a curriculum policy statement. Previously they had to produce a detailed curriculum plan but the aim now is to be more broad-brush in approach.

The policy should set out the principles underpinning the curriculum and reflect the school's commitment to developing all aspects of their pupils' lives. It allows schools to state values and aims as well as the general principles governing their approaches to issues such as inclusion and cross curricular learning. As a guide, it is expected that the policy could normally be set out on a single page of continuous writing. The regulations make the head teacher responsible for preparing the policy and reviewing it annually. The governing body must consider and agree the policy and monitor and review its implementation.

Governors also have curriculum responsibilities beyond the National Curriculum, in areas such as sex education, drug education, careers education and guidance, religious education and collective worship. Information on each is available in schools, from LEAs, and from the DfEE.

In Chapter 7 the phrase 'disapplication of part or all of the National Curriculum' was introduced. A head teacher may, for example, when a pupil has acute learning difficulties, apply for aspects of the National Curriculum to be removed from that pupil's curriculum. This is always done after extensive discussion and consultation with parents. In the unlikely event of a parent wanting to appeal against such a disapplication, it is the governing body who hear the appeal.

All LEAs have to set up procedures, approved by the Secretary of State, for handling complaints about the actions of governing bodies and LEAs on the curriculum. For complaints against the governing body, the first formal stage of the procedure is for the governing body to consider the complaint. If the person with the complaint is still not satisfied after this, he or she can put the complaint to the LEA. Complaints that are just about the LEA's powers or functions only need to be considered by the LEA.

Parents may use the complaints procedure if they believe that either the LEA or the governing body are failing

- to provide the National Curriculum in the school or for a particular child;
- to follow the law on charging for school activities;
- to offer only approved qualifications or syllabuses;
- to provide religious education and daily collective worship;
- to provide the information that they have to provide;
- to carry out any other statutory duty relating to the curriculum; or
- are acting unreasonably in any of the above cases.

Schools and Local Education Authorities now offer training for governors and responsibilities towards the National Curriculum is an area which is thoroughly considered. The DfEE web site has a special part for governors, and national associations also exist to assist those taking on such a key role in schools.

Further sources of information on the National Curriculum

There is now a wide range of publications associated with the National Curriculum. If you type in 'national curriculum' on any of the national bookseller on-line sites, hundreds of books will be listed. The majority are school textbooks. Publishers want to indicate the appropriateness of their books for pupils studying the National Curriculum. Mixed amongst them will be some guides for parents, pupil workbooks to practice tests, and academic studies of the way the National Curriculum is working. In general terms, all the well-known publishers will be producing appropriate material. For parents, the best advice is to seek guidance from teachers in school about the best way their children can be supported. It may be a good thing to provide extra help at home using published materials. It is important, however, that this works in conjunction with school activities and it is very important that children do not feel pressure of a negative kind.

In England the Department for Education and Employment publishes a range of advisory documents and leaflets. Key documents are also published in Bengali, Hindi, Gujerati, Urdu, and Punjabi. A number are also available in Braille and on cassette.

In choosing books, it is important to look at the date of publication to ensure the contents refer to the current version of the National Curriculum. This is particularly true of the books and pamphlets that give examples of National Curriculum tests. Two books that give general advice on assessment issues in the context of the National Curriculum are:

> *Assessment and Children's Learning – Primary*
> *Assessment and Children's Learning – Secondary.*

Both were published in 2001 and were written by E C (Ted) Wragg and published by Routledge/Falmer.

Very useful resources now exist on the internet. Apart from the advantage of cost, information and resources can be kept up-to-date. Examples of useful web sites are listed below.

National sites

All the publications and related materials can be found at the official national curriculum web site: http://www.nc.uk.net

This is a very important site as it gives all the statutory information about all the subjects of the National Curriculum. The official English agency, The Qualifications and Curriculum Authority (often referred to as QCA) which is responsible to the Government for the National Curriculum, runs this site and it is, therefore, the main formal source of information. You will find, in addition to the National Curriculum documentation, schemes of work for implementing the different subjects and examples of pupils' work.

In Northern Ireland the Northern Ireland Network for Education is a useful source of information: http://www.nine.org.uk

In Wales: http://www.accac.org.uk

In England the Department for Education and Employment site contains very useful information, particularly in relation to standards in school: http://www.dfee.gov.uk/

If you want to go straight to the parents' part of the web site, the url is: www.parents.dfee.gov.uk

or for school governors: www.dfee.gov.uk/governor/governor.htm

School governors can also refer to: www.dfee.gov.uk/governor/agog.htm

Other national sites that are of general interest include

The BBC, which is developing a range of digital resources for use in the home and school: http://www.bbc.co.uk

and national newspapers. For example, the *Guardian* has an extensive site devoted to education and community issues: http://www.guardian.co.uk/

The Open University has an ongoing programme that develops resources to help teachers develop their teaching of the National Curriculum: http://www.open.ac.uk/frames.html

There is also a national agency that is concerned with new technologies in schools, The British Educational Communications and Technology Agency: http://www.becta.org.uk

In addition to these national sites, a range of local and school-focussed sites exist. All Local Education Authorities now have web sites. Most schools also have frequently updated sites and a number include examples of pupils' work and activities. Additionally, there are specialist sites that focus on particular aspects or subjects of the National Curriculum. The list below is a small selection from a rapidly changing range of sites.

Primary

National Association of
Primary Education   http://www.nape.org.uk

Special Educational Needs

Becta Inclusion web site   http://inclusion.ngfl.gov.uk
British Dyslexia Association   http://www.bda-dyslexia.org.uk/

English

The National Association of
Teachers of English (NATE)   http://www.actis.co.uk/
                                     projects/pages/nate.html
The English and Media Centre   http://www.englishandmedia.
                                     co.uk

Mathematics

Association of Teachers of
Mathematics   http://www.atm.org.uk
Mathematical Association   http://www.m-a.org.uk/

Science

Association for Science
Education   http://www.ase.org.uk

Design and Technology

Design and Technology
Association   http://www.data.org.uk

Information and Communications Technology

British Computer Society   http://www.bcs.org.uk

National Association for
Co-ordinators and Teachers of IT   http://www.rmplc.co.uk/
orgs/ccitt/

History

The Historical Association   http://www.history.org.uk/

Geography

The Geographical Association   http://www.geography.org.uk/

Art and Design

The National Society for
Education in Art and Design   http://www.nsead.org

The Association of Advisers and
Inspectors in Art and Design
(AAIAD)   http://www.edu.dudley.rmplc.
co.uk/art/aaiad.htm

Music

National Association of
Music Educators (NAME)   http://www.name2.org.uk

Physical Education

Physical Education Association
(PEAUK)   http://www.pea.uk.com

Modern Foreign Languages

Centre for Information in
Language Teaching (CILT)   http://www.cilt.org.uk/

Association for Language
Learning   http://www.languagelearn.co.uk